THE UK SLOW CC RECIPE BOO1

Many easy and delicious dishes for every day of the British tradition. Suitable for beginners and pros.

Daphne White

Introduction

It may seem like fancy new cooking appliances appear every week, but the slow cooker has stood the test of time for its ease and simplicity to use. You don't need to be a gourmet chef to make a slow cooker meal. Just set it and forget it. A slow cooker is an easy way to have a delicious, home-cooked meal waiting for you when you get off work or come home from running errands. It's also perfect for entertaining because you can prepare everything ahead of time and not have to worry about last minute meal prep.

It is the perfect appliance for those who have a busy lifestyle. If you have a full-time job, taking care of kids, or other daily obligations, you can still come home to a nutritious and delicious meal thanks to a slow cooker. Simply put the ingredients in the pot in the morning and let i cook throughout the day. The result is a hot meal waiting for you when you get home.

In this cookbook, you will find a variety of recipes that have been specifically designed for the slow cooker. The recipes are also healthy and nutritious, making them perfect for those who are watching their weight or trying to eat healthier. With just a few minutes of prep time, you can have a delicious and healthy meal that will please the whole family. So, what are you waiting for? Grab your slow cooker and get cooking!

What Is a Slow Cooker?

Slow cookers are plug-in electronic kitchen appliances that use gentle heat to warm up batches of food to a simmer for several hours. They can also be called crockpots. Usually, this common cooking device is used to create dishes that are liquid-based, which allows for a slow and steady heating process.

Often, people leave their slow cookers to cook their meals for the whole day whilst they're away at work. This is partly why they are so popular nowadays, as they provide an easy way to cook without having to be constantly supervised. In addition, most slow cookers have a 'keep warm' setting, meaning that the food will stay at a consistent temperature until it is eaten - ideal for those who want to eat their meal as soon as they get home.

History Behind the Slow Cooker

The slow cooker was invented in the 1940s by Irving Naxon, a Chicago inventor. Naxon was inspired by a story his Jewish grandmother used to tell him about a pot she used to make cholent, a traditional stew eaten by Eastern European Jews on Shabbat. In the story, his grandmother would put all the ingredients for the stew into a pot, and then bury it in the ashes of the fireplace overnight. This way, the food would cook slowly and be ready to eat by the time Shabbat ended.

Naxon thought this was a great idea, and so he set about creating his own version of the pot. The result was the first slow cooker. During this time, women began to work away from home more and more. Because of this, they no longer had time to spend all day in the kitchen cooking dinner for the family.

To overcome this reduction in spare time, women turned to the slow cooker. They could prepare dinner in the morning, pop it into the slow cooker, and leave it to simmer for the whole day whilst they were away at work. When they returned home, they had enough time to finish preparing the food just in time for everybody to sit and enjoy the evening meal together.

It wasn't until the 1970s that large-scale production of slow cookers would begin. With this, they became even more popular. In 1974, slow cookers with removable inserts were first introduced, which made the appliances much easier to clean.

Fast forward to today and slow cookers are much more advanced. Many of them have multiple pre-programmed settings and high-tech heating systems that make slow cooking even simpler and more efficient than ever.

How Should You Use a Slow Cooker?

Using a slow cooker couldn't be easier. Once you have prepared your ingredients, you add them into the cooking pot sitting in the slow cooker, add the lid, set the heat setting, and let the slow cooker do the rest. Further details for slow-cooking specific foods are found below. Use a 3-5 litre slow cooker unless a recipe tells you otherwise.

1. It is really important to never fill a slow cooker to the top. This is because the food needs room to circulate and cook evenly. If the pot is too full, the food will not cook evenly and you may end up with burnt food. The general rule is to fill the pot no more than two-thirds full.

2. Do not remove the lid during cooking. Every time you remove the lid, you let out heat and steam, and this will lengthen the cooking time. If you want to check on the food, use a spoon to peek through the steam vents in the lid. It is not necessary to stir the food unless the recipe specifies.

3. If cooking breads or cakes, always use a silicone or paper liner as the mixture will stick to the side of the pot and be difficult to remove. When making cakes, the slow cooker should be no more than half full to stop the cake from rising too much and becoming overcooked on the top. For breads, the slow cooker should be no more than one-third to one-half full. These guidelines also apply when cooking custards and puddings.

4. For frozen foods, ensure they are completely thawed before adding them to the slow cooker. This is because frozen foods will lower the temperature of the pot, and this will lengthen the cooking time. If you are short on time, you can cook frozen foods directly in the pot, but be aware that they will not cook evenly this way. The best method is to thaw the frozen food in the refrigerator overnight, and then add it to the pot in the morning.

5. The best results are achieved by cooking recipes with the low setting. The extra cooking time is more than worth it to get melt-in-your-mouth meals. If you are pressed for time or if a recipe calls for it, then use the higher heat setting.

6. If you are looking to swap out a conventional oven for a slow cooker in a given recipe, then you will need to adjust the cooking times and amount of liquid used. Slow cookers will need less liquid as very little of the moisture escapes the pot. A recipe which calls for 6-8 hours of cooking time on the low setting will typically take 2-4 hours on the high setting. Cooking in the oven for 15-30 minutes will take 4-6 hours on low, or 1-2 hours on high, using a slow cooker.

Benefits of Using the Slow Cooker

The slow cooker provides several benefits, including the ones below.

It's Simple to Use- Slow cookers are suitable for everybody, regardless of your culinary abilities or cooking experience. Most recipes only need to add ingredients, turn the cooker on, and leave the machine to do its thing for several hours. Easy!

It's Easy to Clean- Slow cookers can be easily wiped down after use and are dishwasher friendly. Cooking your meals in a slow cooker also reduces the use of various pots, pans, and utensils, meaning you have less washed-up to do after dinner.

It Enables Hands-Off Cooking- You can leave slow cookers for hours without needing to check on them regularly. This means you can focus on other activities and errands while you're waiting for your food to cook, making them perfect if you have a hectic schedule.

It Uses Less Energy- Compared to a standard electric oven or hob, slow cookers use less energy, meaning you can save on utility bills. Using the slow cooker twice or thrice a week can significantly cut your expenses in the long run.

It Reduces Your Shopping Bill- As slow cookers enable you to prepare your meals in bulk, it reduces unnecessary spending on several ingredients. You can buy similar ingredients to use in multiple slow cooker recipes, meaning you can buy fewer ingredients for the week ahead, and you can reduce your food wastage. It also cuts the energy costs associated with preparing your meals separately.

It Promotes Healthy Cooking- Preparing your food with a slow cooker provides a healthier alternative to deep-frying or sauteing. Due to the low temperatures, the chance of overcooking your food is low. The essential micronutrients are retained, and the risk of potentially harmful chemicals leaking into your food is reduced.

You Can Make Multiple Portions at Once- Most slow cookers hold large volumes of food, meaning you can prepare multiple portions at once. This saves on time and cost by decreasing the need for multiple ingredients and reducing electricity usage in your home.

Slow cookers are, therefore, perfect for the days when you're cooking for the whole family, having a buffet, hosting a birthday celebration at your house, or meal prepping for the week ahead.

It is Small and Compact- Although most slow cookers can hold large volumes of food, they are usually pretty compact. You can easily keep your device out on the kitchen countertop, neatly tucked away to the side. Alternatively, you can put the slow cooker away in your cupboard to keep your kitchen space clear.

There Are Multiple Varieties- Modern-day technological advancements have brought about a wide variety of different slow cookers. Basic slow cookers usually have low, medium, and high heat settings. You can get more high-tech slow cookers with pre-programmed settings and options that enable you to set a timer on the machine so you can cook your food down to the exact minute.

Tips And Tricks for Slow Cooking

If you're new to slow cooking, the process can seem a bit daunting. After all, you're entrusting your meal to an appliance that you may not be very familiar with. But don't worry, slow cooker recipes are actually very forgiving. As long as you follow these few simple tips, you'll be able to create delicious, home-cooked meals with ease.

Don't Open the Lid. Every time you open the lid, you will need to add 15-20 minutes to the recipe's cooking time. To see what the food looks like inside a round slow cooker, spin the lid to remove any condensation. For an oval slow cooker, jiggle the lid slightly so that the water falls off.

Fill The Slow Cooker Half to Three-Quarters Full. The food will burn if the slow cooker is less than half full, but if filled too full, it may overflow or turn out undercooked food. For soups and stews, you can eyeball the amounts and the recipe will turn out fine.

Brown Food First If You Have Time. With a few exceptions, the upcoming recipes do not call for browning meat before it goes into the appliance. If you have time, browning roasts and chops first in a pan on the stovetop or right in the slow cooker can add to the flavour of the recipe. Browning creates complex compounds that add richness and depth to sauces and meats.

Deglaze If You Have Time. The browned bits left in the slow cooker after cooking meat are full of flavour. If you'd like, when you have removed the food, add about a cup of water or stock and scrape off the browned bits. Transfer this mixture into a saucepan and boil for a few minutes on the stove to make a delicious gravy.

Choose Cheaper Cuts of Meat. Inexpensive cuts of meat (such as rump roast and chuck) are better for slow cooking than expensive cuts (such as rib eye and filet mignon) simply because they have more fat and connective tissue, which melt during the long slow cooking time, adding flavour and making the meat very tender.

Trim Off Excess Fat from Meats. Some fat on meat is good, since that's where the flavour is, but too much fat will make the recipe greasy. Aim for about a quarter inch of fat. Chicken skin should be removed as well (except from a whole chicken), as its texture is unpleasant once slow cooked.

Cut Food into Uniform Pieces. When chopping ingredients, cut everything in similar-size pieces so that everything cooks uniformly.

Put Root Vegetables on The Bottom. Root vegetables require more heat to cook properly, so they should go on the bottom of the slow cooker. More delicate veggies go on top. Place meats, such as a roast, on top of the root veggies. This also helps give more flavour to the veggies, since the fat will melt onto them as they cook.

Add More Fresh Herbs at The End. Long cooking times tend to leach flavour out of herbs. Add more fresh herbs just before you serve the food to boost the flavour. You can also add citrus zest or a squeeze of lemon juice before the cooking time ends.

Add Dairy at The End. Most dairy ingredients, such as milk and sour cream, should be added at the end of the cooking time or they may curdle or split. Where milk is called for, you may use whatever fat content you prefer. Some recipes may call for those ingredients at the start of cooking time, but don't worry—in these cases, the recipe has been developed to take these problems into account.

Which Slow Cooker to Choose?

As the number of households using slow cookers has risen, so has the number of different types of slow cookers for you to choose from. You can find slow cookers from all the popular household kitchen appliance brands, varying in price. Round slow cookers tend to be cheaper and take up less countertop space. Oval slow cookers tend to be larger, allowing enough space for bulky food, such as a whole chicken or pork chops. All slow cookers work in similar ways but differ in features and quality.

You may find a programmable timer to be handy and give you some reassurance if you are away from home. Although, digital slow cookers are more expensive than basic models which are operated manually and with few settings. Typical slow cookers have only low or high settings. Both can be used for cooking and the low setting can also be used to keep food warm. Some slow cookers have an auto setting which starts the cooker on high for several hours and then switches to low until the setting is changed. An indicator light is also an important feature to prevent you from wasting time and food if there is an unexpected power outage.

When looking for a slow cooker for your kitchen, you must first decide on the size or capacity that will suit your needs. The size of the slow cooker does not equate to the amount of food it can cook. Around two-thirds of the stated volume can be used for cooking, as you cannot fill the cooking pot to the top.

The most popular size slow cooker is 3-4.5 litre, suited for a couple or small family. Larger families will need a 5-6.5 litre slow cooker. Large slow cookers have enough capacity for bulk cooking, as you can freeze extra food or leftovers to serve again. A 1.5-3 litre slow cooker is also handy if you host many gatherings or parties as it is perfect for serving sides, snacks, dips, etc.

How Do You Maintain & Clean A Slow Cooker?

Slow cookers are much easier to keep clean nowadays. Most of them have removable components that can be easily washed in your kitchen sink or placed in the dishwasher after use. Here are some of the best maintenance tips to keep your slow cooker looking and functioning as well as it did when you first bought it.

- Allow the slow cooker to cool down after you've used it, then remove the inner compartment (the crock) from the heating element. Along with the lid, wash this inner compartment in the sink, and wipe the outside of the slow cooker if there are any spills or splashes. This ensures no dried food gets stuck on the machine.
- If there are any dried spots of food that you've missed, they can be tough to get off! To help you remove these, take some baking soda or vinegar and dissolve it in warm water. Apply this to the dry spots and use a bristled brush or a cloth to remove them.
- Avoid using harsh scrubbing or very abrasive sponges when cleaning the outer parts of your slow cooker as this could damage the machine.

How to Clean Your Slow Cooker

It's important to clean your slow cooker after every use. This ensures that no tough spots of food dry onto the machine and helps to maintain its function. Follow these steps to give your slow cooker a much-needed deep clean.

For Everyday Cleaning:
You need to get some water, your favourite non-corrosive dish soap, and some baking soda (optional) and follow these steps.

1. Add water to fill ¾ of your slow cooker's insert.
2. Pour in some soap or baking soda (for tougher stains).
3. Plug the cooker in and turn the power on.
4. Set it at low/medium heat for one hour.
5. Pour out the dirty water from the insert and rinse.
6. Leave to dry.

For Deep Cleaning:
1. You can follow the steps above for a deep clean but, instead of dish soap, use a mix of baking soda and vinegar to tackle the tough stains.
2. When cleaning your slow cooker, you can scrub the sides of the insert with a kitchen brush to get rid of any leftover stains. A soft damp cloth can be used to clean the outside, but avoid scrubbing at the slow cooker's surface to prevent scratches.

BREAKFAST

French Toast

Preparation time: 20 minutes
Cooking time: 6-8 hours
Servings: 8
Ingredients:

- 180g brioche loaf, cut into 1-inch cubes
- 15g unsalted butter
- 8 eggs, beaten
- 45g sugar
- 10g vanilla extract
- 5g ground cinnamon
- 5g ground cumin

Directions:

1. Grease your slow cooker pot with some butter, or line it with parchment paper.
2. Whisk together all the ingredients, except the brioche loaf, in a bowl until combined.
3. Layer the bread evenly across the bottom of the slow cooker. Pour the egg mixture evenly until it is fully covered.
4. Cover and cook for 6-8 hours over low heat. Serve it with a drizzle of syrup and some berries, if desired.

Nutrition: Calories: 751; Fat: 40g; Carbs: 47g; Protein: 47g

Breakfast Fruit Compote

Preparation time: 10 minutes

Cooking time: 6-7 hours
Servings: 8-9
Ingredients:

- 340g dried apricots
- 340g pitted dried plums
- 300g mandarin oranges in light syrup, undrained
- 820g sliced peaches in light syrup, undrained
- 60g sultanas
- 10 maraschino or glacé cherries

Directions:

1. Combine all the fixings in your slow cooker.
2. Cover and cook for 6-7 hours on low or for 2 to 3 hours on high. Serve.

Nutrition: Calories: 156; Carbs: 33g; Fat: 1g; Protein: 2g

Cheese And Ham Casserole

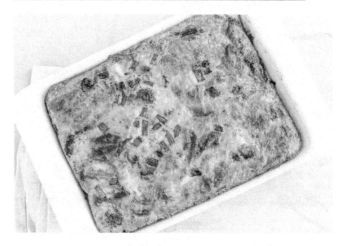

Preparation time: 10 minutes
Cooking time: 8 hours
Servings: 4
Ingredients:

- 8 eggs, beaten
- 200ml of any milk of your choice
- 5g salt
- 2.5g pepper
- 200g ham, pre-cooked and chopped
- 50g cheddar cheese, grated

Directions:

1. Mix the eggs, milk, salt & pepper in a bowl until fully combined. Place half the chopped

ham in your slow cooker and pour the egg mixture over it.

2. Top the mixture with the remaining ham, and evenly spread the grated cheese.
3. Bring the slow cooker onto low heat, add the lid, and leave the casserole to cook overnight for at least 8 hours.
4. The next morning, switch off the slow cooker and allow the mixture to stand for 10 minutes. Serve up in your bowl and top with your favourite condiments.

Nutrition: Calories: 544; Carbs: 16g; Fat: 40g; Protein: 34g

Breakfast Quinoa

Preparation time: 10 minutes
Cooking time: 8 hours
Servings: 4
Ingredients:
- 170g quinoa, rinsed & drained
- 475ml water
- 240g canned coconut milk
- 2 tbsp maple syrup
- ¼ tsp salt
- Splash of milk
- Toppings of your choice, such as berries, honey, or cinnamon

Directions:
1. Add the rinsed quinoa, maple syrup, salt, water and coconut milk into the slow cooker.
2. Put the lid on and cook for 8 hours on low. Serve hot with a splash of milk and toppings of your choice.

Nutrition: Calories: 326; Carbs: 39g; Fat: 17g; Protein: 7g

Apple And Cinnamon Rolls

Preparation time: 10 minutes
Cooking time: 8 hours
Servings: 8
Ingredients:
- 2 cinnamon rolls or cinnamon buns, chopped into quarters
- 2 apples, peeled and diced
- 4 eggs, beaten
- 150ml double cream
- 50g brown sugar
- 5g vanilla extract
- 5g cinnamon

Directions:
1. Grease the inside of your slow cooker and then place the cinnamon roll pieces along the bottom. Add the apples evenly around the rolls.
2. Mix the eggs, cream, sugar, and vanilla extract in your bowl until combined. Pour the egg mixture over the rolls and sprinkle some cinnamon.
3. Bring the slow cooker on low heat, put the lid on top, and cook for 8 hours until the next morning. Serve.

Nutrition: Calories: 110; Carbs: 17g; Fat: 5g; Protein: 1g

Veggie Omelettes

Preparation time: 10 minutes
Cooking time: 1-2 hours & 2 minutes
Servings: 8 servings
Ingredients:

- 8 eggs, beaten
- 100ml any milk of your choice
- 50g parmesan cheese, grated
- 5g dried herbs
- 5g chilli powder
- 1 onion, sliced
- 1 yellow pepper, sliced

Directions:

1. Grease the inner compartment of the slow cooker using butter or oil. Combine the eggs, milk, cheese, and seasoning in a bowl and whisk until combined.
2. Add this mixture to the slow cooker along with the onions and pepper. Cover with its lid and cook for 1-2 hours until the eggs are fully cooked.
3. A couple of minutes before the 1-2 hours is complete, add a sprinkle of cheese on top and cook for a few minutes until the additional cheese has melted. Serve.

Nutrition: Calories: 197; Carbs: 14g; Fat: 10g; Protein: 19g

Strawberries Overnight Oats

Preparation time: 5 minutes
Cooking time: 6-8 hours

Servings: 8 servings
Ingredients:

- 200g rolled oats
- 500ml water
- 500ml of any milk of your choice
- 100g strawberries, hulled
- 150g Greek yoghurt
- 15g chia seeds
- 5g dried cinnamon
- 5g dried nutmeg

Directions:

1. Place all the ingredients into your slow cooker and mix them well.
2. Cover it with the lid and switch it on low heat for 6-8 hours. Serve!

Nutrition: Calories: 243; Carbs: 33g; Fat: 4g; Protein: 12g

Breakfast Hash

Preparation time: 10 minutes
Cooking time: 6-8 hours & 8-9 minutes
Servings: 4
Ingredients:

- 8 to 10 sausages, frozen
- 680g diced potatoes
- 4 medium carrots, sliced
- 2 spring onions
- 4 eggs
- 2 tbsp extra virgin olive oil
- 1 tbsp red wine vinegar
- 1 tsp salt
- ½ tsp ground pepper
- ¼ tsp chilli flakes
- 1 tbsp fresh dill
- 1 tbsp butter
- 2 tbsp crumbled feta
- 2 tbsp maple syrup

Directions:

1. Cook the sausages in a frying pan for 8 to 9 minutes until browned.
2. Combine the potatoes, carrots, spring onions, eggs, and olive oil in a slow cooker.

Stir in the dill, a sprinkle of salt, pepper, and chilli flakes.

3. Arrange the sausages on top and cook for 5 to 6 hours on low. Serve the vegetables on a serving platter sprinkled with feta cheese and topped with sausages.

Nutrition: Calories: 446; Carbs: 42g; Fat: 25g; Protein: 14g

Egg and Sausage Puff

Preparation time: 15 minutes
Cooking time: 2 to 2½ hours
Servings: 6
Ingredients:

- 450g sausage meat
- 6 eggs
- 220g all-purpose baking mix
- 220g shredded Cheddar cheese
- 500ml milk
- ¼ tsp dry mustard (optional)
- Non-stick cooking spray

Directions:

1. Cook the sausage meat in your non-stick skillet for 8 to 9 minutes until browned, breaking it to chunks. Drain excess oil in your paper towel-lined plate.
2. Meanwhile, spray the interior of your slow cooker with non-stick cooking spray. Add all the ingredients and mix well.

3. Cover with a lid and cook within 1 hour on high. Turn to low and cook for 1 to 1½ hours or until fully cooked.

Nutrition: Calories: 446; Carbs: 42g; Fat: 25g; Protein: 14g

Coffee And Banana Baked Bran

Preparation time: 10 minutes
Cooking time: 6-8 hours
Servings: 4
Ingredients:

- 4 ripe bananas, & an extra ½ for toppings
- 500ml of any milk of your choice
- 200ml hot brewed coffee
- 30g brown sugar
- 30g chia seeds
- 200g high bran cereal
- 5g vanilla extract
- 5g dried cinnamon

Directions:

1. Mash up the bananas into a heat-proof bowl and add the milk and coffee. Stir to combine the ingredients fully.
2. Add the remaining ingredients and stir until it forms a consistent mixture. Pour the mixture into the slow cooker. Add some warm water until the machine is around three-quarters full.
3. Cover with the lid, turn the slow cooker onto low heat and simmer overnight for at least 6-8 hours.
4. Top with the ½ sliced banana and a sprinkle of sugar before serving.

Nutrition: Calories: 493; Carbs: 43g; Fat: 19g; Protein: 25g

Breakfast Sweet Potato Bake

Preparation time: 10 minutes
Cooking time: 8 hours & 10-15 minutes
Servings: 4
Ingredients:
- 300g sweet potato, peeled & chopped
- 1 (400g) can of chopped tomatoes
- 1 (400g) can of butter beans
- 2 rashers bacon, chopped
- 200ml of any milk of your choice
- 30g cheese

Directions:
1. Add all the fixings to your slow cooker, excluding the cheese. Set the slow cooker to low heat and cover it with the lid for 8 hours.
2. The next morning, grate your cheese and add it to the slow cooker. Leave to cook for 10-15 minutes until the cheese has melted. Serve.

Nutrition: Calories: 654; Carbs: 65g; Fat: 22g; Protein: 29g

Chia Seed Jam Overnight Oats

Preparation time: 15 minutes
Cooking time: 8 hours & 7-8 minutes
Servings: 8
Ingredients:
- 150g strawberries, hulled
- 45g chia seeds
- 45g flax seeds
- 45g sugar
- 200g rolled oats
- 800ml water
- 500ml of any milk of your choice
- 5g dried cinnamon

Directions:
1. Add the strawberries to a pan and cook them over medium heat for 5 minutes until the fruit starts to break down. Add the chia seeds, flax seeds, and sugar, then stir well.
2. Continue to cook over low heat for 2-3 minutes and set aside.
3. Place the remaining fixings into the slow cooker, then add the jam mixture. Cook on low heat for 8 hours or overnight. Serve with berries and an extra sprinkle of cinnamon on top, if desired.

Nutrition: Calories: 353; Carbs: 52g; Fat: 14g; Protein: 16g

Turkish Breakfast Eggs

Preparation time: 10 minutes
Cooking time: 5-6 hours & 2 minutes
Servings: 4
Ingredients:

- 1 slice of sourdough bread, cubed
- 2 onions, sliced
- 1 red pepper, chopped
- 1 small red chilli, finely sliced
- 1 tbsp olive oil
- 4 eggs
- 8 cherry tomatoes
- 2½ tbsp skimmed milk
- Small bunch of parsley, finely chopped
- 4 tbsp natural yoghurt to serve

Directions:

1. Grease the inside of the slow cooker.
2. Heat the oil in your pan, and cook the chilli, pepper, and onions for 2 minutes until they soften. Add it to your slow cooker, and stir in the bread and tomatoes. Season to taste.
3. Whisk the eggs, milk, and parsley in your bowl, and pour this over.

4. Cook on low heat for 5-6 hours. Serve with a spoonful of natural yoghurt.

Nutrition: Calories: 165; Carbs: 13g; Fat: 8g; Protein: 9g

Breakfast Frittata Casserole

Preparation time: 10 minutes
Cooking time: 2-3 hours & 2 minutes
Servings: 8
Ingredients:

- 2 tsp olive oil
- 140g baby kale, rinsed & pat dry
- Non-stick spray or oil to grease the slow cooker if needed
- 170g roasted red peppers, diced
- 1 sliced spring onion
- 140g crumbled feta
- 8 eggs, beaten
- ½ tsp multi-purpose seasoning
- Ground black pepper to taste

Directions:

1. Heat your pan with the oil over medium to high heat. Sauté the kale for 1 to 2 minutes until it has softened.
2. Grease your slow cooker with non-stick spray and add the cooked kale. Add the red pepper and spring onion. Beat the eggs and stir into the slow cooker.
3. Season with the multi-purpose seasoning and black pepper, then sprinkle it with feta. Cook on low for 2 to 3 hours and serve hot.

Nutrition: Calories: 166; Carbs: 5g; Fat: 12g; Protein: 10g

POULTRY RECIPES

Chicken Cacciatore

Preparation time: 10 minutes
Cooking time: 7-8 hours
Servings: 4
Ingredients:
- 1kg chicken thighs
- 2 (800g) cans of chopped tomatoes
- 250g mushrooms, quartered
- 100g pitted kalamata olives
- 60ml red wine or chicken broth
- 3 garlic cloves, minced
- 2 bell peppers, chopped
- 10g basil

Directions:
1. Season both sides of all the chicken thighs with salt and pepper.
2. Add the seasoned chicken thighs, garlic, bell peppers, mushrooms, tomatoes, and red wine to the slow cooker—season with salt, pepper, and basil.
3. Cover with its lid and cook on low for 7-8 hours. Once cooked, add the pitted olives and mix them well. Serve.

Nutrition: Calories: 392; Carbs: 11g; Fat: 14g; Protein: 51g

Sweet And Sticky Chicken Wings

Preparation time: 5 minutes
Cooking time: 6 hours
Servings: 4
Ingredients:
- 30ml soy sauce
- 30ml balsamic vinegar
- 45ml honey
- 15ml water
- 5ml hot sauce
- Zest 1 lemon or lime
- 600g chicken wings
- 60g cornstarch
- 15g sesame seeds
- 15g dried mixed herbs

Directions:
1. Mix the soy sauce, balsamic vinegar, honey, hot sauce, and lemon or lime zest in a bowl until fully combined.
2. Arrange the chicken wings in your slow cooker and pour in the wet mixture. Stir well. Add the lid to your slow cooker and cook the wings on low heat for 6 hours.
3. In a bowl, mix the cornstarch with 15ml water. Add this into the slow cooker 10 minutes before the 6 hours is complete.
4. Remove the chicken wings, then coat in the sesame seeds and dried mixed herbs. Serve.

Nutrition: Calories: 387; Carbs: 22g; Fat: 16g; Protein: 21g

Chicken Marsala

Preparation time: 10 minutes
Cooking time: 5 hours & 38-40 minutes
Servings: 4
Ingredients:

- 700g boneless chicken breasts
- 250g mushrooms, sliced
- 150ml dry marsala wine
- 60ml double cream
- 30g cornstarch
- 2 garlic cloves, minced
- 30g parsley
- 15 ml olive oil
- 5g basil
- 5g thyme
- Salt & pepper to taste
- 100ml water

Directions:

1. Flavour the chicken with salt, pepper, and herbs.
2. Heat a skillet with olive oil over medium-high heat. Cook the chicken for 3-4 minutes per side until lightly browned.
3. Transfer the seared chicken, garlic, wine, and mushrooms to the slow cooker. Cover and cook on low for 5 hours.
4. In your small bowl, whisk the water and cornstarch together until blended.
5. Remove the chicken breasts, pour in the cornstarch mixture and double cream. Whisk to combine with the wine.
6. Arrange the chicken in your slow cooker, cover, and then cook on high for 20-30 minutes or until the sauce thickens. Top with parsley and serve.

Nutrition: Calories: 492; Carbs: 11g; Fat: 22g; Protein: 53g

Chicken Chasseur

Preparation time: 10 minutes
Cooking time: 7 hours & 14 minutes
Servings: 2
Ingredients:

- 4 chicken thighs, skin-on, bone-in
- 200g baby chestnut mushrooms, halved
- 200g chopped tomatoes
- 200ml white wine
- 400ml chicken stock
- 15g tomato puree
- 30ml olive oil
- 2 shallots, chopped
- 1 bay leaf
- 2 thyme sprigs
- 2 garlic cloves, crushed

Directions:

1. Heat the oil in your frying pan over medium-high. Cook the chicken within 3-4 minutes per side until lightly browned. Transfer to a plate
2. In your same pan, add the shallot and cook within 2 minutes until tender. Add the mushrooms plus garlic, then cook for 4 minutes.
3. Add the tomato puree, tomatoes, wine, thyme, bay leaf, and tomatoes. Simmer for 4 minutes.
4. Transfer the mixture to the slow cooker, add the chicken, cover, and cook for 7 hours on low. Serve.

Nutrition: Calories: 488; Carbs: 15g; Fat: 26g; Protein: 29g

Chicken Noodle Soup

Preparation time: 15 minutes
Cooking time: 6 hours & 10-12 minutes
Servings: 8

Ingredients:

- 2 chicken stock cubes
- 500g boneless chicken breast, chopped
- 1 onion, chopped
- 1 clove garlic, peeled and crushed
- 2 carrots, peeled and chopped
- 1 leek, chopped
- 50g mange tout
- 5g dried herbs
- 4 nests of dry noodles
- Boiling water, as needed

Directions:

1. Dissolve the chicken stock cubes in boiling water as stated on the packet and pour them into the slow cooker. Add the remaining ingredients, except the noodles, and stir to combine.
2. Cover and cook on low for 6 hours.
3. Around 15 minutes before the 6 hours is complete, boil some water in a pan and cook the noodles for 10-12 minutes until soft.
4. Serve the noodles up in your bowls and pour the chicken broth mixture on top.

Nutrition: Calories: 478; Carbs: 20g; Fat: 8g; Protein: 36g

Roast Chicken with Carrots

Preparation time: 5 minutes
Cooking time: 6 hours
Servings: 4
Ingredients:

- 1 medium whole chicken, giblets removed, rinsed
- 2 carrots, halved
- 1 bay leaf
- 1 onion, peeled and sliced
- 30g butter, softened
- 100ml chicken broth

Directions:

1. Add butter, carrots, onion, chicken, broth, plus bay leaf to your slow cooker.
2. Cover and cook on low for 6 hours. Serve.

Nutrition: Calories: 497; Carbs: 7g; Fat: 30g; Protein: 41g

Sweet Potato Turkey Chilli

Preparation time: 10 minutes
Cooking time: 4 hours & 7 minutes
Servings: 6
Ingredients:

- 450g minced turkey
- 400ml chicken broth
- 400g sweet potato puree or mash
- 1 (400g) can of green chilli peppers
- 1 (400g) can of cannellini beans
- 180g sour cream
- 1 onion, diced
- 5g garlic powder
- 5g chilli powder
- 5g cumin

Directions:

1. Heat a skillet over medium heat. Cook the ground turkey and onions for 5-6 minutes until the meat is lightly browned, breaking the minced turkey.
2. Drain any excess water from the pan, then transfer the onions and turkey to the slow cooker.
3. Pour the chicken broth and sweet potato puree into the slow cooker. Add the green chilli peppers—season with salt, pepper, garlic powder, chilli powder, and cumin.
4. Cover, then cook on low for 4 hours. Add the can of beans and cook for 1 more hour. Serve with sour cream.

Nutrition: Calories: 537; Carbs: 60g; Fat: 16g; Protein: 42g

Turkey Casserole

Preparation time: 15 minutes
Cooking time: 6 hours & 15 minutes
Servings: 4
Ingredients:

- 400g turkey breast, pre-cooked and chopped

- 1 onion, chopped
- ½ red pepper, sliced
- 4 eggs, beaten
- 200ml of any milk of your choice
- 30g plain flour
- 5g dried chilli flakes
- 30g cheddar cheese, grated

Directions:
1. Add the turkey, onion, and red pepper to the slow cooker.
2. Whisk the eggs, milk, flour, and chilli flakes in your bowl, then pour into the slow cooker. Mix it well
3. Switch the slow cooker onto low-medium heat, add the lid, and cook for 6 hours. Open, and sprinkle the grated cheese on top.
4. Place the lid back and cook for 15 minutes until the cheese has melted. Serve.

Nutrition: Calories: 434; Carbs: 42g; Fat: 15g; Protein: 29g

Turkey Stew

Preparation time: 10 minutes
Cooking time: 5-6 hours & 5 minutes
Servings: 6
Ingredients:
- 675g turkey breast, cubed
- 200g salsa
- 1 (400g) can bean with chilli
- 1 (400g) can of chopped tomatoes
- 3 garlic cloves

- 1 onion, chopped
- 1 red pepper, chopped
- 1 green pepper, chopped
- ¼ tsp salt
- ½ tsp ground cumin
- 1½ tsp chilli powder
- 2 tsp oil

Directions:
1. In a frying pan, brown the turkey for 5 to 6 minutes. Add to the slow cooker and stir in the remaining ingredients.
2. Cook on low for 5 to 6 hours until the turkey is cooked through. Serve.

Nutrition: Calories: 238; Carbs: 17g; Fat: 4g; Protein: 33g

Turkey Meatballs

Preparation time: 10 minutes
Cooking time: 5 hours & 5 minutes
Servings: 4
Ingredients:
- 500g tomato passata
- 450g minced turkey
- 2 celery sticks, finely diced
- 1 garlic clove, crushed
- 2 garlic cloves, thinly sliced
- 2 carrots, finely diced
- 1 onion, finely chopped
- Pinch of paprika
- 2 tbsp chopped parsley
- 4 tbsp porridge oats
- 1 tbsp rapeseed oil

Directions:
1. In a frying pan, cook the celery, onion, garlic, and carrots in the oil for a minute. Stir in the passata and parsley, then transfer them into the slow cooker.
2. Place the turkey into your large bowl. Add the oats, paprika, garlic, plus plenty of black pepper, then mix everything with your hands.

3. Make the meatballs out of this mixture. Spray your non-stick pan with oil and cook the meatballs for 5 to 6 minutes until brown.
4. Add it to your slow cooker and cook on low for 5 hours. Serve.

Nutrition: Calories: 260; Carbs: 21g; Fat: 5g; Protein: 29g

Pulled Turkey

Preparation time: 10 minutes
Cooking time: 6-8 hours
Servings: 5
Ingredients:
- 560g turkey breast
- 480ml water
- 120ml sweet pickle juice
- Powdered onion soup or sauce mix
- 2 tbsp canned diced jalapenos
- 120ml fat-free Greek yoghurt
- 1 tbsp yellow mustard
- ¼ tsp pepper

Directions:
1. Add the turkey to the slow cooker.
2. Mix the pickle juice with the soup mix and jalapenos in a bowl, then transfer over the turkey. Cook on low for 6 to 8 hours. Remove the turkey and shred it. Set aside.
3. Strain the cooking juices, reserving about 120ml. Stir together the cooking juices, yoghurt, mustard, and pepper. Pour over turkey and toss to coat before serving.

Nutrition: Calories: 339; Carbs: 40g; Fat: 4g; Protein: 36g

Turkey Breast with Wine and Bacon

Preparation time: 10 minutes
Cooking time: 3-4 hours & 30 minutes
Servings: 2-4
Ingredients:
- 16 rashers smoked streaky bacon
- 2 turkey breast fillets
- 500ml chicken stock
- 150ml dry white wine
- 2 carrots, sliced
- 15g dried porcini mushrooms
- 1 onion, halved and thickly sliced
- 2 tbsp fresh thyme leaves, + extra to serve
- 1 tbsp sunflower oil
- 2 bay leaves
- 2 tbsp plain flour

Directions:
1. Lay a piece of string twice the length of the turkey on a board.
2. Arrange another 4 lengths of string and tie it around the width of your turkey fillet across the first string, winding them around the first string once, so they do not move much.
3. Place 8 rashers of the bacon across the string in the same direction as the 4 strings.
4. Overlap the rashers slightly. Scatter with 1 tablespoon of thyme and add a generous amount of black pepper.
5. Lay a turkey fillet on top of the bacon and then wrap the bacon around it using the strings. Tie the strings snuggly, but not too tight. Cut any excess string off with scissors.
6. Cook the fillet in the oil in a frying pan, then place it in the slow cooker. Repeat with the second turkey fillet.
7. Add the carrots and onions to the pan, and fry until starting to brown. Put the contents of the frying pan in the slow cooker, then add the mushrooms and bay.
8. Lay the turkey on top. Tip the wine and stock into the frying pan and quickly bring them to

a boil before pouring them into the slow cooker. Cook on low for 3 to 4 hours.

9. Take out the turkey, then wrap it in foil to keep warm. Stir the flour into 4 tablespoons of water to make a paste.

10. Transfer the cooking liquid into your saucepan and mix it with the flour paste until it thickens. Serve the turkey with the gravy and vegetables of your choice.

Nutrition: Calories: 297; Carbs: 7g; Fat: 12g; Protein: 35g

BEEF, PORK, AND LAMB RECIPES

Beef Tacos

Preparation time: 10 minutes
Cooking time: 4-5 hours
Servings: 8
Ingredients:

- 1 (400g) can of chopped tomatoes
- 15ml chipotle sauce
- 10g ground cumin
- ¼ tsp salt
- 3 cloves garlic, peeled and finely chopped
- 1 onion, thinly sliced
- 400g beef, minced

Directions:

1. Combine the chopped tomatoes, chipotle sauce, cumin, and salt in a bowl. Stir in the garlic, onion, and beef.
2. Transfer the mixture to your slow cooker and cook on high heat for 4-5 hours until the beef is cooked. Serve.

Nutrition: Calories: 365; Carbs: 25g; Fat: 17g; Protein: 21g

Beef Pot Roast

Preparation time: 10 minutes
Cooking time: 6-7 hours
Servings: 6-8
Ingredients:

- 1 (1.8 to 2.3 kg) beef chuck roast
- 1 garlic clove, cut in half
- 1 carrot, chopped
- 1 rib celery, chopped
- 1 small onion, sliced
- 175 ml sour cream
- 3 tbsp flour
- 125 ml dry white wine
- Salt & pepper to taste

Directions:

1. Rub the roast with garlic, then season with salt and pepper. Transfer to your slow cooker, then add the carrots, celery, and onion.
2. Combine the sour cream, flour, and wine in a bowl. Pour it into the slow cooker. Cover, and cook on low for 6 to 7 hours. Serve.

Nutrition: Calories: 210; Carbs: 30g; Fat: 4g; Protein: 14g

Beef Teriyaki

Preparation time: 10 minutes
Cooking time: 8 hours
Servings: 6
Ingredients:

- 1kg rump steak, sliced
- 150ml beef stock
- 50ml soy sauce
- 50ml honey
- 50ml rice wine vinegar
- 5g crushed ginger
- 5g garlic, crushed
- 2.5g black pepper, ground

Directions:

1. Add all the fixings to your slow cooker.
2. Cover and cook on low for 8 hours. Serve.

Nutrition: Calories: 328; Carbs: 27g; Fat: 9g; Protein: 35g

Beef Goulash

Preparation time: 10 minutes
Cooking time: 7 hours & 14 minutes
Servings: 8
Ingredients:

- 2kg stewing beef, cut into chunks
- 4 peppers (red, green, yellow), cut into chunks
- 3 garlic cloves, minced
- 2 onions, chopped
- 4 tomatoes, chopped
- 15g sweet smoked paprika
- 10g hot smoked paprika
- 10g caraway seeds
- 60g tomato puree
- 30g flour
- 300ml sour cream
- 400ml beef stock
- 45ml olive oil

Directions:

1. Heat 30 ml of olive oil in the frying pan. Once hot, add the beef and cook for 5 minutes until evenly browned. Set aside.
2. In the same pan, add the reserved oil. Add the onions and cook for 4 minutes. Add the garlic and pepper, then cook for 4 minutes.
3. Add the smoked paprika, caraway seeds, and tomato puree. Cook for 1 minute, stirring often, and transfer to the slow cooker.
4. Add browned beef, tomatoes, and beef stock. Put on the lid and cook on low for 7 hours.

Nutrition: Calories: 581; Carbs: 17g; Fat: 32g; Protein: 54g

Beef Stroganoff

Preparation time: 20 minutes
Cooking time: 5 hours & 30 minutes
Servings: 8
Ingredients:
- 900g beef silverside, sliced into cubes

- 450g flat egg noodles, cooked & drained
- 240g sour cream
- 200ml beef broth
- 200ml white wine
- 200g mushrooms, sliced
- 150g cream cheese (softened)
- 40g all-purpose flour
- 1 onion, diced
- 15ml Worcestershire sauce

Directions:
1. Add the cubed beef, Worcestershire sauce, white wine, sliced mushrooms, and onions in the greased slow cooker.
2. Add most of the beef broth, but reserve roughly 50ml—season with salt and lots of black pepper. Stir to combine fully.
3. Cover and cook on low within 5 hours. About 30 minutes before cooking time is complete, whisk together the flour, cream cheese, sour cream, and beef broth.
4. Gently stir into the slow cooker. Do not cover it with the lid—Cook for 30 minutes on high. Serve the creamy beef sauce over egg noodles.

Nutrition: Calories: 639; Carbs: 49g; Fat: 26g; Protein: 46g

Savoury Pepper Steak

Preparation time: 15 minutes
Cooking time: 8-10 hours & 20 minutes
Servings: 6
Ingredients:

- 1 (680g) beef topside or silverside steak, cut ½-inch thick
- 60g flour + 3 tbsp, divided
- ½ tsp salt
- ¼ tsp pepper
- 1 medium onion, chopped or sliced
- 1 garlic clove, minced
- 2 large green peppers, sliced into ½-inch strips, divided
- 2 (400g) cans of whole tomatoes

- 1 tbsp beef flavour base or 1 beef bouillon or stock cube
- 1 tbsp soy sauce
- 2 tsp Worcestershire sauce
- 3 tbsp water

Directions:

1. Combine 60g flour, salt, and pepper in a bowl. Toss with beef until well coated. Transfer it in your slow cooker with half the green pepper, garlic, and onions. Mix well.
2. Combine the tomatoes, beef base, soy sauce, and Worcestershire sauce. Pour into slow cooker. Cover, and cook on low for 8 to 10 hours.
3. One hour before serving, turn to high and stir in the remaining green pepper.
4. Combine 3 tablespoons of flour and water until a smooth paste forms. Stir into the slow cooker, cover, and cook until thickened. Serve.

Nutrition: Calories: 170; Carbs: 7g; Fat: 8g; Protein: 17g

Hoisin Pork Ribs

Preparation time: 10 minutes
Cooking time: 8 hours & 30 minutes
Servings: 6
Ingredients:
- 1.7kg pork ribs
- 2 tbsp tomato purce

- 125ml soy sauce
- 75ml white wine
- 4 cloves of garlic, crushed
- 225g caster sugar
- 235ml hoisin sauce
- ½ tsp Chinese five-spice powder
- 2 tsp chilli-garlic sauce
- Salt & ground black pepper to taste

Directions:
1. Preheat the oven to 180°C. Put the ribs on a baking tray and season with salt and pepper. Bake for 30 minutes until lightly browned.
2. Stir the remaining ingredients in a bowl. Once cooked, put the ribs in the slow cooker, and pour over the sauce.
3. Cook on low for 8 hours, turning halfway through, until the ribs are tender. Serve.

Nutrition: Calories: 928; Carbs: 55g; Fat: 45g; Protein: 69g

Pulled Pork

Preparation time: 10 minutes
Cooking time: 6 hours
Servings: 8
Ingredients:
- 1 onion, finely chopped
- 60g ketchup
- 45g tomato paste
- 45ml BBQ sauce
- 30ml apple cider vinegar
- 15g BBQ seasoning
- 5g smoked paprika
- 5g garlic powder
- 5g mustard powder
- 600g pork, excess fat removed
- 2.5g salt
- 2.5g black pepper

Directions:
1. Combine the onion, ketchup, tomato paste, BBQ sauce, apple cider vinegar, and spices in a bowl.
2. Chop the pork into pieces and rub each piece into the sauce mixture until fully covered.

3. Add the pork to the slow cooker with a pinch of salt and black pepper. Cover with the lid, then cook on high heat for 6-8 hours until the pork is cooked through.
4. Removed the pork and shred it. Serve in a bun along with some salad and extra BBQ sauce.

Nutrition: Calories: 411; Carbs: 27g; Fat: 19g; Protein: 30g

Fruited Pork

Preparation time: 10 minutes
Cooking time: 4-6 hours
Servings: 6
Ingredients:
- 1 (900g) boneless pork loin roast
- ½ tsp salt
- ¼ tsp pepper
- 240g mixed dried fruit
- 120ml apple juice

Directions:
1. Place the pork in your slow cooker. Sprinkle with salt and pepper. Top with fruit and pour the apple juice on top.
2. Cover and cook on low for 4 to 6 hours or until pork is tender. Serve.

Nutrition: Calories: 432; Carbs: 54g; Fat: 15g; Protein: 17g

Pork Belly

Preparation time: 10 minutes
Cooking time: 4 hours & 10 minutes
Servings: 5-6
Ingredients:
- 1 (1.2kg) pork belly, rind trimmed& cut into 3 long strips
- 2 onions, sliced
- 3 garlic cloves, crushed
- 3 tsp sea salt
- 1 tbsp soy sauce
- 1 thumb-sized piece of root ginger, finely grated

Directions:
1. Stir the garlic, soy sauce, salt, and ginger in a bowl, then rub it into the pork belly. Put the onion in the slow cooker and the pork on top—Cook for 4 hours on high.
2. Take the pork out and transfer it to a frying pan along with a couple of tablespoons of the cooking juices.
3. Cook over high heat for 8 to 10 minutes, turning regularly until the pork is browned and the juices have evaporated. Serve with potatoes, vegetables, and gravy.

Nutrition: Calories: 540; Carbs: 4g; Fat: 40g; Protein: 39g

Pork in Peanut Sauce

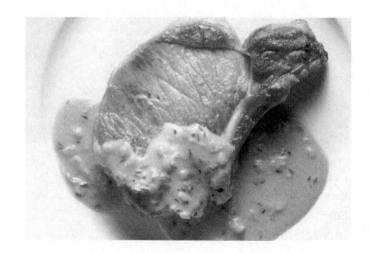

Preparation time: 10 minutes
Cooking time: 5-6 hours
Servings: 2
Ingredients:

- 450g boneless pork chops
- 45g smooth peanut butter
- 150ml chicken stock
- 3 cloves garlic, finely chopped
- 1 red pepper, thinly sliced
- 35ml soy sauce
- 1½ tbsp honey
- 1 tbsp fresh ginger, finely chopped
- 1½ tsp chillies, crushed

Directions:

1. Add all the fixings to your slow cooker and stir well.
2. Cook for 5 to 6 hours on low. Remove the pork and shred it. Put it back again and continue to cook until heated through. Serve.

Nutrition: Calories: 372; Carbs: 24g; Fat: 15g; Protein: 37g

Lamb Lettuce Wraps

Preparation time: 20 minutes
Cooking time: 5-6 hours
Servings: 8
Ingredients:

- 900g lamb chunks
- 200g chunky salsa
- 100g apricot preserves
- 6 tbsp dry red wine
- 2 tbsp ras el hanout
- 2 tsp chilli powder
- ½ tsp garlic powder
- 1 cucumber, thinly sliced
- Lettuce leaves to serve

Directions:

1. Mix the lamb, salsa, preserves, ras el hanout, chilli powder, garlic powder, and 4 tablespoons of red wine in a bowl. Transfer to the slow cooker and cook for 5 to 6 hours on low.

2. Remove the lamb and shred it. Skim the fat from the slow cooker and strain the remaining juices.
3. Put the lamb and cooking juices back in the slow cooker. Stir in remaining wine, and heat until warm. Serve the lamb in lettuce leaves topped with cucumber.

Nutrition: Calories: 221; Carbs: 13g; Fat: 8g; Protein: 24g

Lamb Tagine

Preparation time: 10 minutes
Cooking time: 4-8 hours & 15 minutes
Servings: 4
Ingredients:

- 950g lamb, cut into chunks
- 3 medium carrots, chunks
- 1 large onion, chopped
- 30g dried cherries
- 1 sweet potato, chopped
- 1 tsp ground cumin
- 2 tsp ras-el-hanout
- 1 tbsp tomato purée
- ½ tsp honey
- 1 tbsp olive oil
- 1 chicken or lamb stock cube or stock pot
- ½ bunch coriander, chopped
- Couscous, to serve

Directions:

1. Brown the lamb in the oil over medium to high heat for 8 minutes. Tip it into the slow cooker once done.
2. Cook the onion in the same frying pan within 5 minutes until starting to soften.
3. Tip in the carrots and spices and stir together. Add the tomato puree, 250ml of water, and the stock, and stir together before tipping into the slow cooker.
4. Add the potato, cherries, honey, and another 500ml of water to the slow cooker—Cook for 8 hours on low or 4 hours on high. Serve with a sprinkling of coriander and couscous.

Nutrition: Calories: 649; Carbs: 17g; Fat: 45g; Protein: 42g

Lamb Shawarma

Preparation time: 20 minutes
Cooking time: 5 hours
Servings: 8
Ingredients:
For the wrap:
- 2kg lamb shoulder
- 8-10 large wraps or flatbread pieces
- 300ml beef or lamb broth
- 100ml water
- 250g shredded lettuce
- 3 garlic cloves, minced
- 2 Roma tomatoes, chopped into small quarter-slices
- 1 small cucumber, chopped into small quarter-slices
- 45ml olive oil
- 30ml lemon juice
- 15g cumin
- 15g coriander
- 5g paprika

For the sauce:
- 300ml plain Greek yoghurt
- 2 garlic cloves, minced
- 15g chopped mint
- 15g dill
- 10ml lemon juice

Directions:
1. Mix the 3 minced garlic, olive oil, lemon juice, cumin, coriander, and paprika in a bowl. Mix until it forms a paste, then lather all over the lamb shoulder.
2. Add the broth and water to the slow cooker. Carefully insert the lamb shoulder, then season with salt and pepper. Cover, then cook on high for 5 hours.
3. Mix the yoghurt, minced garlic, chopped mint, dill, lemon juice, salt and pepper in your small bowl. Cool in the fridge until the lamb is cooked.
4. Slice or shred the cooked lamb and feel free to mix it with any of the leftover juices in the slow cooker.
5. Arrange the shawarma by filling each wrap with lamb, minted yoghurt, shredded lettuce, chopped tomatoes, and cucumber. Roll into neat wraps and serve.

Nutrition: Calories: 623; Carbs: 36g; Fat: 23g; Protein: 65g

Lamb Shanks with Red Wine Gravy

Preparation time: 10 minutes
Cooking time: 8 hours & 15 minutes
Servings: 4
Ingredients:
- 4 lamb shanks
- 250ml light red wine
- 500ml stock, vegetable, chicken, or lamb

- 1 large onion, finely chopped
- 2 medium carrots, chopped
- 3 garlic cloves, peeled
- 2 tbsp olive oil
- 2 tbsp tomato purée
- 2 thyme sprigs
- 2 bay leaves
- 2 tbsp plain flour
- 1 bunch parsley, leaves chopped

Directions:

1. Put half the oil in your frying pan and cook the lamb on all sides. Transfer to the slow cooker once done; you may need to work in batches.
2. Add the remaining oil and fry the onion until it softens and becomes translucent. Mix in the tomato puree and flour, then cook again for 1 minute.
3. Add the red wine and increase the heat until it boils. Stir constantly until the sauce is smooth. Tip the mixture into the slow cooker.
4. Add the stock, bring it back to a boil, and transfer it to the slow cooker.
5. Add the garlic, carrots, bay leaves, thyme, and parsley to the slow cooker, and cook for 8 hours on low, turning the lamb once. Serve.

Nutrition: Calories: 547; Carbs: 15g; Fat: 32g; Protein: 37g

FISH & SEAFOOD RECIPES

Fish Au Gratin

Preparation time: 10 minutes
Cooking time: 2 hours & 3 minutes
Servings: 6 servings
Ingredients:

- 1.3kg cod or tilapia fillets
- 300ml milk
- 250g shredded cheddar cheese
- 60g butter
- 30g grated parmesan cheese
- 45g all-purpose flour
- 5ml lemon juice
- 5g mustard
- 5g chopped chives (optional)
- 1 lemon (optional)

Directions:
1. Heat a saucepan with butter over medium heat. Add the flour and mustard—season with salt and pepper. Stir to combine for 2-3 minutes until you have a smooth paste.
2. Pour in the milk one-third at a time, constantly stirring so the sauce can thicken.
3. Add the cheddar cheese and stir it to melt into the sauce. Once all the cheese is in, add the lemon juice.
4. Layer the white fish at the bottom of the slow cooker. Pour in all the cheese sauce until the fish is completely and evenly coated—top everything with a sprinkling of parmesan cheese.
5. Cover and then cook on high for 2 hours. Serve with a topping of chopped chives and lemon wedges on the side.

Nutrition: Calories: 481; Carbs: 7g; Fat: 26g; Protein: 54g

Fish Stew with Chickpeas

Preparation time: 10 minutes
Cooking time: 2-3 hours & 15 minutes
Servings: 4
Ingredients:

- 550g white fish fillets
- 125ml tomato passata
- 3 garlic cloves, crushed
- 3 tomatoes, cut into chunks
- 1 onion, finely chopped
- 400g tin of chickpeas, rinsed
- 1 or 2 tbsp oil
- 2 tbsp plain flour
- Freshly chopped parsley
- Salt, pepper, turmeric, and cumin to taste

Directions:

1. Fry the onion in the pan with oil for 10 to 15 minutes until soft.
2. Mix the flour, spices, and seasoning in a bowl, and coat the fish in the flour mixture. Put the fish in the slow cooker, then add the remaining ingredients.
3. Cook for 2 to 3 hours on low until the fish is opaque and flaky.

Nutrition: Calories: 454; Carbs: 28g; Fat: 18g; Protein: 39g

Slow Cooked Lobster

Preparation time: 9 minutes
Cooking time: 1 hour
Servings: 2
Ingredients:

- 900g lobster tails, cut in half
- 30g unsalted butter, melted
- A pinch of salt
- 60ml white wine
- 120ml water

Directions:
1. Put all the ingredients into the slow cooker.
2. Cover with its lid and cook on low for 1 hour. Mix it well and serve.

Nutrition: Calories: 324; Carbs: 8g; Fat: 21g; Protein: 15g

Fish Curry

Preparation time: 10 minutes
Cooking time: 2 hours
Servings: 2
Ingredients:
- 455g salmon fillets, cut into bite-sized pieces
- 1 curry leaves
- 7.5ml olive oil
- 2.5g red chilli powder
- ½ small yellow onion, diced
- 1 garlic clove, minced
- 15g curry powder
- 5g ground cumin
- 5g ground coriander
- 2.5g ground turmeric
- 240ml unsweetened coconut milk
- 128g tomato, diced
- ½ Serrano pepper, seeded and diced
- 7.5ml fresh lemon juice

Directions:
1. Add all the fixings to your slow cooker. Cover and cook on low for 2 hours.
2. Mix it well and serve.

Nutrition: Calories: 216; Carbs: 7g; Fat: 22g; Protein: 29g

Chorizo and Prawn Orzo

Preparation time: 10 minutes
Cooking time: 2 hours & 25 minutes
Servings: 4
Ingredients:
- 125g chorizo, diced
- 800ml chicken or vegetable stock
- 1 onion, chopped
- 1 stalk of celery, diced
- 5 garlic cloves, crushed
- 2 tbsp extra-virgin olive oil
- 125ml white wine
- 200g cherry tomatoes, quartered
- 200g orzo
- 400g raw peeled king prawns
- A handful of parsley, finely chopped
- 1 lemon to serve

Directions:
1. Turn the slow cooker on high.
2. Add the chorizo, chicken or vegetable stock, onion, celery, garlic, olive oil, white wine, and cherry tomatoes to your slow cooker. Cook it on high for 2 hours.
3. Stir in the pasta and sprinkle on the prawns. Cook for 20 to 25 minutes until the pasta is soft and the prawns are pink.
4. Stir in the chopped parsley with some seasoning and serve with lemon wedges.

Nutrition: Calories: 449; Carbs: 41g; Fat: 17g; Protein: 25g

Citrus Salmon with Cream Sauce

Preparation time: 20 minutes
Cooking time: 2 hours & 12 minutes
Servings: 4
Ingredients:

For the salmon:
- 1kg salmon fillets
- 250ml vegetable broth
- 60g melted butter
- 3 garlic cloves, minced
- 3 shallots, minced
- 2 lemons, zested & chop 1 of the lemons
- 1 orange, zested & sliced into halves
- 5g thyme
- 2.5g cayenne pepper

For the sauce:
- 150ml double cream
- 100ml water or chicken broth

Directions:
1. Line the slow cooker with parchment paper, then create a layer of lemon slices at the bottom and add the salmon.
2. Mix the melted butter, minced garlic, shallots, cayenne pepper, and thyme in a bowl. Season it with salt and pepper.
3. Add most lemon and orange zest, saving a pinch of each to use in the sauce. Mix.

4. Pour the butter, zest, and spice mixture over the salmon in the slow cooker. Pour the vegetable broth around the salmon. Cover and then cook on low for 2 hours.
5. About 15-20 minutes before the salmon is done, make the cream sauce. Heat a small saucepan over medium heat.
6. Add the cream, water or chicken broth, juice of one whole lemon, and juice of half an orange. Stir to combine fully.
7. Adjust to low heat, cover, and simmer for 7-10 minutes. Adjust medium-high heat and add the remaining lemon and orange zest—season with salt and pepper.
8. Cook for 1-2 more minutes until the sauce has thickened. Serve the salmon with sauce on the side or top.

Nutrition: Calories: 615; Carbs: 36g; Fat: 30g; Protein: 55g

Paprika Shrimp

Preparation time: 10 minutes
Cooking time: 50 minutes
Servings: 4
Ingredients:

- 910g raw shrimp, peeled and deveined
- 5g paprika
- 6 garlic cloves, sliced
- 1.2g red pepper flakes
- 180ml olive oil
- Black pepper & salt, to taste

Directions:
1. Combine the oil, red pepper flakes, black pepper, paprika, garlic, and salt in your slow cooker. Cover and then cook on high for 30 minutes. Add the shrimp and stir well.
2. Cover and cook on high for 10 minutes. Stir well, cover again, and cook for 10 minutes more. Serve.

Nutrition: Calories: 247; Carbs: 5g; Fat: 6g; Protein: 14g

Slow Cooked Mussels

Preparation time: 10 minutes
Cooking time: 2 hours
Servings: 2
Ingredients:

- 910g mussels, cleaned and de-bearded
- 30g butter
- 1 medium yellow onion, diced
- 1 garlic clove, minced
- 2.5g rosemary, dried and crushed
- 240ml homemade chicken broth
- 30g fresh lemon juice
- 120g sour cream
- Salt & black pepper, to taste

Directions:
1. Add all the ingredients, except the cream, into the slow cooker.
2. Cover with its lid and cook on high for 2 hours. Stir in the cream and mix it well. Serve.

Nutrition: Calories: 245; Carbs: 2g; Fat: 16g; Protein: 32g

Poached Salmon with Lemon and Herbs

Preparation time: 10 minutes
Cooking time: 2 hours & 30 minutes
Servings: 6
Ingredients:
- 950g skin-on salmon

- 250ml white wine
- 480ml water
- 1 shallot, sliced
- 1 lemon, sliced
- 1 bay leaf
- 1½ tsp salt
- 1½ tsp black peppercorns
- Salt & pepper to taste
- 5 to 6 sprigs of fresh herbs, such as tarragon, dill, or Italian parsley
- Lemon wedges, sea salt, and olive oil to serve

Directions:
1. Mix the wine, water, lemon, shallots, herbs, bay, peppercorns, and salt in the slow cooker—Cook for 30 minutes on high.
2. Season the salmon with salt and pepper. Put the skin-side down in the bottom of the slow cooker. Cook on low for 2 hours until the salmon is opaque and flaky.
3. Drizzle it with olive oil, then season it with coarse salt. Serve with lemon wedges.

Nutrition: Calories: 359; Carbs: 4g; Fat: 20g; Protein: 31g

Curried Shrimp

Preparation time: 13 minutes
Cooking time: 2 hours & 30 minutes
Servings: 2
Ingredients:

- 15ml olive oil
- 1 medium onion, diced
- 2.5g cumin, ground

- 7.5g red chilli powder
- 5g ground turmeric
- A pinch of salt
- 2 medium tomatoes, diced
- 60ml water
- 795g medium shrimp, peeled and deveined
- 15ml fresh lemon juice
- 32g fresh cilantro, diced

Directions:
1. Add all the fixings, except shrimp, into the slow cooker. Cover and cook on low for 2 hours.
2. Stir well, add the shrimp, and cook on low for 30 minutes. Serve warm.

Nutrition: Calories: 287; Carbs: 6g; Fat: 29g; Protein: 5g

Prawn and Fennel Risotto

Preparation time: 10 minutes
Cooking time: 2 hours
Servings: 4
Ingredients:
- 300g risotto rice
- 1 large fennel bulb, sliced
- 2 tbsp olive oil
- 1 shallot, sliced
- 1 garlic clove
- 2 preserved lemons, chopped seeds discarded
- 150ml white wine
- 1-litre vegetable stock
- 300g raw king prawns
- 40g Pecorino cheese, grated

Directions:
1. Cook the fennel in the pan with oil for 5 minutes. Add the shallot and cook for another 5 to 8 minutes until almost cooked through.
2. Tip in the garlic and rice, and cook for 5 minutes, stirring constantly. Add the white wine and let it boil for 30 seconds.
3. Add to the slow cooker and stir in the stock—season to taste. Cook on high for 1

hour and 30 minutes, then stir in the prawns and lemons.
4. Cook for a further 10 minutes until the prawns are cooked. Stir through the cheese and add a little extra stock if needed.

Nutrition: Calories: 502; Carbs: 67g; Fat: 12g; Protein: 23g

Salmon Bisque

Preparation time: 10 minutes
Cooking time: 6-8 hours & 12 minutes
Servings: 4
Ingredients:
- 750ml fish stock or clam juice, divided
- 770g peeled chopped potatoes
- 50g chopped onion
- 25g finely chopped celery
- 55g finely chopped carrot
- 1 tbsp tomato paste
- 1½ tsp dried dill weed
- 1¼ –1½ tsp dry mustard
- 200–300g skinless salmon steaks
- 1.3-litre whole milk, divided
- 2 tbsp cornstarch
- 2–3 tsp lemon juice
- salt & white pepper, to taste

Directions:
1. Combine the stock, vegetables, tomato paste, dill weed, plus dry mustard in a slow cooker.
2. Cover and cook on low for 6 to 8 hours. Add the salmon steaks and 500ml milk during the

last 15 minutes. Remove the salmon, flake it into small pieces and reserve.

3. Process the soup in your blender until smooth. Return it to the slow cooker.
4. Add the flaked salmon to your slow cooker—cover and cook on high for 10 minutes.
5. Stir in combined remaining milk and cornstarch, stirring for 2 to 3 minutes. Drizzle it with lemon juice, then season with salt and white pepper.

Nutrition: Calories: 213; Carbs: 22g; Fat: 6g; Protein: 20g

VEGETARIAN RECIPES

Green Lentil Curry

Preparation time: 10 minutes
Cooking time: 4 hours & 5 minutes
Servings: 6
Ingredients:

- 400ml coconut milk
- 1 (400g) can of chopped tomatoes
- 400g green lentils
- 200g plain yoghurt
- 5 garlic cloves, diced
- 1 onion, diced
- 15ml olive oil
- 5g cumin
- 5g coriander
- 5g turmeric powder
- 5g cayenne pepper
- 500ml water

Directions:

1. Heat a small skillet over medium-low heat. Cook the onion and garlic for 4-5 minutes until lightly golden.
2. Add the turmeric powder, cayenne pepper, coriander, and cumin. Season with salt and stir for 20-30 seconds.
3. Transfer the cooked garlic, onion, and spices to the slow cooker. Pour in the coconut milk, chopped tomatoes, water, and lentils. Mix well.
4. Cover and then cook on high for 4 hours. Serve.

Nutrition: Calories: 461; Carbs: 52g; Fat: 19g; Protein: 22g

Butternut Squash Mac & Cheese

Preparation time: 15 minutes
Cooking time: 4 hours & 3 minutes
Servings: 6
Ingredients:

- 500g macaroni or other short pasta, cooked & drained
- 350g butternut squash, cubed
- 200ml vegetable broth
- 150g shredded sharp cheddar cheese
- 150g grated gouda or gruyere cheese
- 150ml milk
- 1 garlic clove, minced
- 1 onion, minced
- 1.25g red pepper flakes
- 1.25g thyme
- 100g grated parmesan cheese (optional)

Directions:

1. Heat olive oil in your skillet on medium heat. Cook the garlic and onion for 2-3 minutes until fragrant and tender.
2. Add the cooked garlic, onion, broth, and butternut squash to the slow. Stir together. Cover and then cook on high for 4 hours.
3. Transfer the squash to your blender, and blend until paste forms.
4. Add the milk plus cheese, flavour with the seasonings, and herbs. Stir to combine fully.
5. Add the cooked pasta to the cheesy squash sauce. Serve with grated parmesan cheese.

Nutrition: Calories: 124; Carbs: 74g; Fat: 20g; Protein: 31g

Sweet-Sour Cabbage

Preparation time: 20 minutes
Cooking time: 3-5 hours
Servings: 6
Ingredients:

- 1 medium-head red or green cabbage, shredded
- 2 onions, chopped
- 4 tart apples, pared, quartered
- 80g raisins
- 60ml lemon juice
- 60ml cider or apple juice
- 3 tbsp honey
- 1 tbsp caraway seeds
- ¼ tsp allspice
- ½ tsp salt

Directions:
1. Combine all the fixings in your slow cooker.
2. Cook on high for 3 to 5 hours until the cabbage is soft. Serve.

Nutrition: Calories: 66; Carbs: 9g; Fat: 2g; Protein: 3g

'No Chicken' Casserole

Preparation time: 20 minutes
Cooking time: 3-4 hours
Servings: 8
Ingredients:

- 1 (400g) block of extra-firm tofu, drained & pressed to remove excess water
- 1 onion, chopped
- 1 carrot, peeled and chopped
- 1 leek, chopped
- 10g brown sugar
- 1 (400g) can of coconut milk
- 1 (400g) can of chopped tomatoes
- 5g curry powder
- 5g chilli powder
- 5g black pepper

Directions:

1. Add all the fixings to the slow cooker. Add the tofu once it is firm enough.
2. Cover and cook on low for 3-4 hours. Serve.

Nutrition: Calories: 299; Carbs: 15g; Fat: 17g; Protein: 27g

Cranberry-Orange Beets

Preparation time: 15 minutes
Cooking time: 3-7 hours & 30 minutes
Servings: 6
Ingredients:

- 900g medium beetroots, peeled and quartered
- ½ tsp ground nutmeg
- 240 ml cranberry juice
- 1 tsp orange peel, finely shredded (optional)
- 2 tbsp butter
- 2 tbsp sugar
- 4 tsp cornflour

Directions:

1. Place the beets in the slow cooker, and sprinkle with nutmeg. Add the cranberry juice and orange peel. Dot it with butter. Cover, and cook on low for 6 to 7 hours or on high for 3 to 3½ hours.
2. In a small bowl, combine sugar and cornflour. Remove 120ml of cooking liquid and stir into the cornflour.
3. Stir mixture into slow cooker. Cover with its lid and cook on high within15 to 30 minutes.

Nutrition: Calories: 299; Carbs: 15g; Fat: 17g; Protein: 27g

Chickpea, Sweet Potato, And Spinach Curry

Preparation time: 15 minutes
Cooking time: 4 hours & 15 minutes
Servings: 4
Ingredients:

- 15ml olive oil
- 1 onion, sliced
- 1 (400g) can of chickpeas, drained & rinsed
- 30g curry powder
- 200g sweet potato, peeled and diced
- 1 bell pepper, sliced
- 1 (400g) can of chopped tomatoes
- 1 (200g) can of coconut milk
- 2 cloves garlic, peeled and chopped
- 5g salt
- 4 handfuls fresh spinach

Directions:

1. Place the oil, onion, chickpeas, and curry powder in the slow cooker and stir well. Add the remaining ingredients, except the spinach on top. Do not stir.
2. Cover with its lid and cook for 4 hours until the chickpeas are slightly softened.
3. Add the spinach and cover with the lid again. Cook for 15 minutes until the spinach has wilted. Stir well and serve.

Nutrition: Calories: 369; Carbs: 45g; Fat: 14g; Protein: 20g

Ratatouille

Preparation time: 15 minutes
Cooking time: 3 hours
Servings: 4
Ingredients:

- 150g white potato
- 1 onion, sliced
- 2 cloves garlic, peeled and crushed
- 2 courgettes, sliced
- 1 red pepper, sliced
- 1 zucchini, sliced
- 1 (400g) can of chopped tomatoes or tomato pasta sauce
- 10g dried herbs
- 60g cheese (any type), grated

Directions:

1. Add all the fixings into your slow cooker and mix well. Cover, and cook on medium heat for 3 hours until the potatoes are soft.
2. Top with some grated cheese before serving.

Nutrition: Calories: 300; Carbs: 28g; Fat: 8g; Protein: 19g

Stuffed Bell Peppers

Preparation time: 5 minutes
Cooking time: 4 hours
Servings: 3

Ingredients:

- 6 red or yellow bell peppers, sliced the top & seeded
- 1 (400g) can of black beans
- 1 (400g) can of diced tomatoes
- 180g uncooked quinoa
- 80g shredded cheddar cheese
- 60g corn
- 1 onion, diced
- 2.5g cumin
- 2.5g chilli powder
- 150g sour cream or plain Greek yoghurt (optional)

Directions:
1. In a bowl, combine the quinoa, black beans, corn, onion, diced tomatoes, chilli powder, cumin, and three-quarters of the shredded cheddar cheese. Season with salt and mix together.
2. Spoon into the peppers until full. Pour about 100ml into the greased slow cooker.
3. Place the stuffed peppers into your slow cooker, cover with its lid, and cook on low for 4 hours. Serve with sour cream or plain yoghurt as a topping.

Nutrition: Calories: 455; Carbs: 52g; Fat: 21g; Protein: 20g

Caramelized Onions

Preparation time: 10 minutes
Cooking time: 12 hours
Servings: 6-8
Ingredients:
- 6 to 8 large Vidalia or other sweet onions, peeled
- 4 tbsp butter or margarine
- 1 (285g) can of chicken or vegetable stock

Directions:
1. Place the onions in your slow cooker and pour the butter and stock over. Cook on low for 12 hours and serve.

Nutrition: Calories: 70; Carbs: 3g; Fat: 5g; Protein: 1g

Stewed Tomatoes

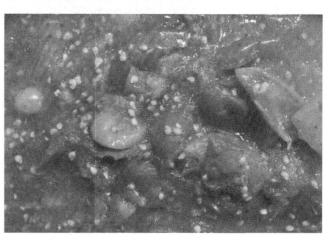

Preparation time: 10 minutes
Cooking time: 3-4 hours
Servings: 12
Ingredients:
- 500g low-sodium canned tomatoes
- 50g sugar
- 1 tsp salt
- Dash of black pepper
- 2 tbsp butter
- 140g bread cubes

Directions:
1. Place the tomatoes in your slow cooker. Sprinkle with sugar, salt, and pepper.
2. Lightly toast bread cubes in melted butter in a pan over low heat. Spread it over the tomatoes.
3. Cover, and cook on high for 3 to 4 hours. Serve.

Nutrition: Calories: 188; Carbs: 28g; Fat: 8g; Protein: 2g

Vegetable Curry

Preparation time: 15 minutes
Cooking time: 5 hours & 5 minutes
Servings: 6
Ingredients:
- 400ml vegetable broth
- 1 (400g) can of chickpeas
- 200ml coconut milk
- 200g cauliflower, cut into florets

- 200g sweet potato, sliced into cubes
- 3 yellow or red bell peppers, diced
- 30g tomato paste
- 15ml olive or canola oil
- 2 garlic cloves, minced
- 1 onion, diced
- 10g ground coriander
- 5g turmeric powder
- 2.5g cayenne pepper
- 2.5g ground ginger

Directions:
1. Heat a pan with oil over medium-high heat. Cook the diced onions for 4-5 minutes until translucent and lightly golden.
2. Add the minced garlic, coriander, turmeric, cayenne pepper, ground ginger, and tomato paste. Stir to combine and cook for 1 minute or until the garlic is fragrant.
3. Transfer the mixture of onions, garlic, and spices to the slow cooker. Pour the vegetable broth, coconut milk, and all the chopped vegetables.
4. Mash the chickpeas with a fork and transfer them into the slow cooker—season with salt and pepper. Stir well, cover and cook on low for 5 hours. Serve.

Nutrition: Calories: 406; Carbs: 59g; Fat: 13g; Protein: 18g

Courgette Casserole

Preparation time: 10 minutes
Cooking time: 4-6 hours
Servings: 6
Ingredients:
- 220-320g thinly sliced courgette
- 1 medium onion, diced
- 2 large carrots, shredded
- 1 (305g) can 98% fat-free cream of celery soup
- 1 (305g) can of condensed cream chicken soup
- ¼ tsp salt
- Fat-free cooking spray

Directions:
1. Spray your slow cooker with cooking spray. Mix all the fixings in your slow cooker.
2. Cover, and cook on high for 4 to 6 hours or until vegetables are tender. Serve.

Nutrition: Calories: 406; Carbs: 59g; Fat: 13g; Protein: 18g

Mushroom Wild Rice

Preparation time: 10 minutes
Cooking time: 0 hours
Servings: 12
Ingredients:
- 525ml water
- 200ml beef stock
- 1 (400g) can of French onion soup
- 275g mushrooms, chopped
- 110g butter, melted
- 190g uncooked brown rice
- 160g uncooked wild rice

Directions:
1. Mix all the fixings in your slow cooker.
2. Cover, and cook on high for 7 to 8 hours. Serve.

Nutrition: Calories: 188; Carbs: 24g; Fat: 8g; Protein: 4g

PASTA RECIPES

Chicken Lasagne

Preparation time: 15 minutes
Cooking time: 4 hours & 10 minutes
Servings: 4
Ingredients:

- 15ml coconut oil
- 1 onion, sliced
- 1 garlic clove, peeled and crushed
- 1 (400g) jar of Alfredo sauce
- 400g boneless chicken breast, pre-cooked and diced
- 1 (400g) can of chopped tomatoes
- 90g tomato paste
- 8 sheets lasagne
- 75g cheddar cheese, grated

Directions:
1. Heat the oil in your frying pan and add the onion and garlic. Cook for 8-10 minutes until they become fragrant.
2. Spread a quarter layer of Alfredo sauce across your slow cooker, then add a quarter of cooked onion and garlic and 100g of chicken.

3. Layer 2 lasagne sheets over the top, 1/3 canned chopped tomatoes and 30g tomato paste. Repeat until all the ingredients have been used, with the final layer being 2 lasagne sheets.
4. Cook on low for 4 hours with the lid on. Around 15 minutes before the 4 hours are complete, sprinkle most of the grated cheese evenly on top of the lasagne. Serve.
5. Serve up with some chips or salad and top with the remaining cheese.

Nutrition: Calories: 654; Carbs: 43g; Fat: 28g; Protein: 34g

Tortellini with Broccoli

Preparation time: 10 minutes
Cooking time: 2½ to 3 hours
Servings: 4
Ingredients:

- 120ml water
- 1 (740g) jar of your favourite pasta sauce divided
- 1 tbsp Italian seasoning
- 1 (255g) package of frozen spinach and cheese tortellini
- 1 (450g) package of frozen broccoli florets

Directions:

1. Mix the water, pasta sauce, and seasoning in a bowl. Pour one-third of the sauce into your slow cooker. Top with all the tortellini.
2. Pour one-third of the sauce over the tortellini, and top with broccoli. Pour the remaining sauce over the broccoli.
3. Cook on high for 2½ to 3 hours or until broccoli and pasta is tender but not mushy.

Nutrition: Calories: 240; Carbs: 26g; Fat: 11g; Protein: 10g

Pork Ragu Pasta

Preparation time: 20 minutes
Cooking time: 5 hours & 15 minutes
Servings: 6
Ingredients:

- 1kg boneless pork shoulder, sliced into big chunks
- 2 (800g) cans of chopped tomatoes
- 600g pappardelle or fettuccine pasta, cooked & drained
- 150ml chicken broth
- 100ml red wine
- 50g grated parmesan cheese
- 5 garlic cloves, minced
- 3 medium carrots, finely diced
- 1 onion, finely diced
- 1 bay leaf
- 30g tomato paste
- 15ml olive oil
- 5g sugar
- 5g thyme
- 5g oregano

Directions:

1. Heat your large pan with olive oil over medium-high heat. Put in the pork, and flavour it with salt plus pepper. Cook for 2-3 minutes on each side until the meat is lightly browned.
2. Add the onions and cook for 3-4 minutes. Add the garlic and chopped onions. Stir, then cook for another 1-2 minutes until the garlic

is fragrant. Pour the wine into the pan and boil for 5 minutes.
3. Stir in the chopped tomatoes, tomato paste, chicken broth, sugar, thyme, and oregano. Season again with salt and pepper. Stir well and let it simmer.
4. Transfer it to the slow cooker and add the bay leaf. Cover with its lid and cook on high for 4 to 5 hours.
5. Discard the bay leaf and shred the pork. Serve the pasta with the pork sauce, and grated parmesan cheese on top.

Nutrition: Calories: 359; Carbs: 14g; Fat: 11g; Protein: 49g

Easy Spaghetti

Preparation time: 10 minutes
Cooking time: 3-8 hours
Servings: 8
Ingredients:

- 900g beef mince, browned and drained
- 50g chopped onions
- 2 cloves garlic, minced
- 2 (425g) cans of tomato sauce
- 2 to 3 tsp Italian seasoning
- 1½ tsp salt
- ¼ tsp pepper
- 2 (110g) cans of sliced mushrooms, drained
- 1.4-litre tomato juice
- 1 (450g) dry spaghetti broken into 4 to 5-inch pieces
- Grated Parmesan cheese

Directions:

1. Combine all the ingredients except spaghetti and cheese in the 4-litre slow cooker.
2. Cover with its lid and cook on low for 6 to 8 hours or on high for 3 to 5 hours. During the last 30 minutes, adjust to high heat and add the spaghetti. Stir well. Sprinkle it with Parmesan cheese before serving.

Nutrition: Calories: 200; Carbs: 45g; Fat: 1g; Protein: 3g

Creamy Chicken Pasta with Sun-Dried Tomatoes

Preparation time: 10 minutes
Cooking time: 3 hours & 25 minutes
Servings: 4 servings
Ingredients:

- 500ml chicken broth
- 500g boneless chicken thighs cut into bite-sized pieces
- 250g short pasta of choice
- 220g cream cheese
- 140g sun-dried tomatoes (including oil)
- 50g grated parmesan cheese
- 3 garlic cloves, finely diced
- 1 red onion, finely diced
- 15g Italian seasoning

Directions:

1. Pour the chicken broth into the greased slow cooker. Flavour it with pepper, salt, and Italian seasoning.
2. Add the chicken thighs, onion, and garlic. Cover with the lid, then cook on high for 3 hours or until chicken is cooked through.
3. Add the pasta and sun-dried tomatoes and cook on high for 25 more minutes.
4. Add the parmesan and cream cheese to the slow cooker. Stir into the pasta and broth until fully combined. Serve with any extra parmesan cheese.

Nutrition: Calories: 768; Carbs: 54g; Fat: 44g; Protein: 37g

Chicken Broccoli Alfredo

Preparation time: 20 minutes
Cooking time: 1-2 hours & 30 minutes
Servings: 4
Ingredients:

- 1 (230g) package of noodles or spaghetti
- 100g fresh or frozen broccoli
- 450g uncooked boneless, skinless chicken breasts, cubed
- 1 (305g) can of cream of mushroom soup
- 55g shredded mild Cheddar cheese

Directions:

1. Cook the noodles as stated in the package directions. Add the broccoli before the cooking time ends. Drain well.
2. Sauté the chicken in a non-stick pan for 5 minutes until no longer pink in the centre.
3. Combine all the fixings in the slow cooker. Cover with its lid and cook on low for 1 to 2 hours until the cheese is melted.

Nutrition: Calories: 348; Carbs: 24g; Fat: 17g; Protein: 18g

Red Beans and Pasta

Preparation time: 15 minutes
Cooking time: 3-4 hours
Servings: 6-8
Ingredients:

- 3 (425g) cans of chicken or vegetable stock
- ½ tsp ground cumin

- 1 tbsp chilli powder
- 1 garlic clove, minced
- 230g spiral pasta, uncooked
- Half a large green pepper, diced
- Half a large red pepper, diced
- 1 medium onion, diced
- 1 (425g) can of red beans, rinsed and drained
- Chopped fresh parsley for serving
- Chopped fresh coriander for serving

Directions:
1. Combine the stock, cumin, chilli powder, and garlic in your slow cooker.
2. Cover, and cook on high until the mixture comes to a boil. Add the pasta, vegetables, and beans. Stir together well.
3. Cover with its lid and cook on low for 3 to 4 hours. Add the parsley or coriander before serving.

Nutrition: Calories: 260; Carbs: 25g; Fat: 15g; Protein: 7g

Cheesy Rigatoni

Preparation time: 20 minutes
Cooking time: 3-4 hours & 8 minutes
Servings: 6-8
Ingredients:
- 680g beef mince or bulk Italian sausage
- 1 medium onion, chopped
- 1 green pepper, chopped
- Half a box of rigatoni, cooked
- 1 (200g) jar of sliced mushrooms, drained
- 85g sliced pepperoni
- 1 (454g) jar of pizza sauce
- 285g Mozzarella cheese, shredded
- 285g Cheddar cheese, shredded

Directions:
1. Cook the minced beef and onions in your saucepan for 6 to 8 minutes. Drain excess oil.
2. Layer half of each beef mince and onions, green pepper, noodles, mushrooms, pepperoni, pizza sauce, and both cheeses in your slow cooker.

3. Repeat the layers until all your fixings are used. Cover, and cook on low for 3 to 4 hours. Serve.

Nutrition: Calories: 345; Carbs: 34g; Fat: 13g; Protein: 24g

Turkey Stuffed Giant Pasta

Preparation time: 10 minutes
Cooking time: 3-6 hours & 10 minutes
Servings: 8
Ingredients:
- 1-litre tomato pasta sauce
- 950g minced turkey
- 28 giant pasta shells
- 3 cloves of garlic
- 1 red onion, diced
- ½ tbsp garlic powder
- 1 tbsp dried basil
- 1 tbsp dried parsley
- 1 tbsp dried oregano
- 1 tbsp avocado oil
- 375g ricotta
- 120g fresh diced spinach
- 85g mozzarella
- Salt & pepper to taste

Directions:
1. Heat the avocado oil in your pan over high heat and cook the onions for 2 minutes until softened. Add the garlic and cook for 30 seconds.
2. Add the turkey and cook for 5 minutes until no longer pink. Add the spinach and wilt for 1 to 2 minutes.
3. Mix the ricotta, turkey mixture, herbs, and seasonings in a bowl. Stuff each shell with the mixture.
4. Put half the pasta sauce in the slow cooker and put the shells on top. Pour half the remaining sauce, then another layer of the pasta shells. Finish with the rest of the sauce.
5. Cook for 3 hours on high or for 6 hours on low. Sprinkle over the mozzarella, and let the pasta stand for 5 minutes until the cheese melts before serving.

Nutrition: Calories: 205; Carbs: 12g; Fat: 6g; Protein: 27g

Pasta with Lentil Sauce

Preparation time: 15 minutes
Cooking time: 3-10 hours
Servings: 4-6
Ingredients:

- 25g chopped onions
- 65g chopped carrots
- 60g chopped celery
- 400g diced tomatoes in liquid
- 225g tomato sauce
- 85 to 115g dried lentils, rinsed and drained
- ½ tsp dried oregano
- ½ tsp dried basil
- ½ tsp garlic powder
- ¼ tsp crushed red pepper flakes
- 800g hot angel-hair pasta, cooked & drained

Directions:

1. Mix all the fixings except pasta in your slow cooker. Cover, and cook on low for 8 to 10 hours or on high for 3 to 5 hours.
2. Place the cooked pasta in your large bowl and pour lentil sauce over the top. Toss to combine and serve.

Nutrition: Calories: 276; Carbs: 58g; Fat: 3g; Protein: 11g

Two-Cheeses Macaroni

Preparation time: 10 minutes
Cooking time: 2 hours
Servings: 6
Ingredients:

- 115g butter, cut into pieces
- 200g macaroni, uncooked
- 220g shredded sharp cheese, divided
- 680g small-curd cottage cheese
- 600ml boiling water

Directions:

1. Place the butter in the bottom of the slow cooker. Add the uncooked macaroni, 170g shredded cheese, and cottage cheese. Stir together until well mixed.
2. Pour the boiling water over everything. Do not stir; cover with its lid and cook on high for 2 hours.
3. Stir well, and sprinkle with remaining shredded cheese. Let it stand for 10 to 15 minutes before serving.

Nutrition: Calories: 210; Carbs: 22g; Fat: 8g; Protein: 11g

Spaghetti with Beef and Veggies

Preparation time: 15 minutes
Cooking time: 4-6 hours
Servings: 6
Ingredients:

- 50g chopped onions
- 150g chopped green peppers
- 1 tbsp butter
- 1 (800g) can of tomatoes with juice
- 1 (110g) can mushroom, chopped and drained
- 1 (65g) can slice ripe olives, drained
- 2 tsp dried oregano
- 450g beef mince, browned and drained
- 340g spaghetti, cooked and drained
- 1 (305g) can cream of mushroom soup
- 120ml water
- 160g shredded Cheddar cheese
- 20g grated Parmesan cheese

Directions:

1. Sauté the onions and green peppers in your pan with butter for 3 minutes until tender. Add the tomatoes, mushrooms, olives, oregano, and beef.

2. Simmer it for 10 minutes and transfer it to your slow cooker. Add the spaghetti and mix well.

3. Combine the soup and water, then add them to your slow cooker. Sprinkle with cheeses, cover, and cook on low within 4 to 6 hours. Serve.

Nutrition: Calories: 399; Carbs: 13g; Fat: 26g; Protein: 27g

SOUPS AND STEWS

Minestrone

Preparation time: 20 minutes
Cooking time: 8 hours & 20 minutes
Servings: 6

Ingredients:
- 900ml vegetable broth
- 1 (400g) can of chopped tomatoes
- 1 (400g) can of red kidney beans, drained
- 1 (400g) can of cannellini beans, drained
- 150g green beans, sliced
- 150g ditalini pasta or macaroni
- 60g spinach
- 50g grated parmesan cheese
- 30g tomato paste
- 4 garlic cloves, diced
- 2 medium carrots, quarter-sliced
- 2 stalks of celery, sliced
- 1 courgette, quarter-sliced
- 1 white onion, diced
- 1 bay leaf
- 5g oregano

Directions:
1. Add all the chopped vegetables to the slow cooker. Add the remaining ingredients except for kidney beans, cannellini beans, spinach, and pasta—season well with salt and pepper.
2. Cover and then cook on low for 7-8 hours. Add the beans, pasta, and spinach. Cover with its lid and cook on high for 20 minutes or until pasta is cooked. Serve with any remaining parmesan cheese.

Nutrition: Calories: 112; Carbs: 38g; Fat: 5g; Protein: 42g

Butternut Squash Soup

Preparation time: 15 minutes
Cooking time: 6-8 hours & 10 minutes
Servings: 8

Ingredients:
- 15ml oil
- 1 onion, chopped
- 1 butternut squash, peeled and cubed
- 2 vegetable stock cubes
- 2.5g black pepper
- 2.5g dried garlic granules

Directions:
1. Heat the oil in your frying pan and cook the onion for 8-10 minutes until it is lightly browned and fragrant.
2. Add the onions to the slow cooker with the remaining fixings. Pour 400ml water, cover, and cook on low heat for 6-8 hours.
3. Once cooked, remove the soup from the slow cooker. Place half of the soup in your blender, and pulse until the mixture is smooth and creamy.
4. Combine the two halves of the soup once again and stir well. Serve!

Nutrition: Calories: 280; Carbs: 16g; Fat: 9g; Protein: 6g

Tempeh Noodle Soup

Preparation time: 10 minutes
Cooking time: 4 hours
Servings: 4

Ingredients:
- 15ml coconut oil
- 1 onion, sliced
- 2 vegetable stock cubes
- 1 (400g) block tempeh, diced
- 2 carrots, peeled and chopped
- 100g baby sweetcorn
- 100g mange tout
- 4 nests of wholewheat noodles, cooked & drained
- 5g salt
- 5g black pepper

Directions:
1. Heat the coconut oil in your frying pan and add the onion. Cook over medium heat within 8-10 minutes until it softens.
2. Dissolve the vegetable stock cubes in boiling water according to the packet instructions and pour this into the slow cooker.
3. Place the onions in the slow cooker along with all the remaining ingredients. Cover, and cook on medium for 4 hours.
4. Once ready, serve up into 4 even portions and add a sprinkle of salt and pepper to each dish.

Nutrition: Calories: 346; Carbs: 29g; Fat: 14g; Protein: 31g

Broccoli & Cheese Soup

Preparation time: 10 minutes
Cooking time: 4 hours & 15 minutes
Servings: 6
Ingredients:
- 900ml vegetable broth
- 250ml double cream
- 350g grated cheddar cheese
- 50g all-purpose flour
- 2 medium heads of broccoli, cut into bite-sized florets
- 2 carrots, shredded
- 1 yellow onion, diced

Directions:
1. Add all the chopped vegetables to the slow cooker.
2. In a bowl, whisk the vegetable broth and the flour until combined. Pour into the slow cooker. Season with salt plus pepper, cover with its lid and cook on high for 3-4 hours.
3. Before cooking time is up, remove the lid. Add the double cream and grated cheese. Stir to combine and cook for an additional 15 minutes. Serve.

Nutrition: Calories: 477; Carbs: 18g; Fat: 35g; Protein: 22g

Rich Salmon Soup

Preparation time: 10 minutes
Cooking time: 4 hours
Servings: 2

Ingredients:

- 455g salmon fillets
- 15ml coconut oil
- 128g carrot, peeled and diced
- 64g celery stalk, diced
- 64g yellow onion, diced
- 128g cauliflower, diced
- 475ml homemade chicken broth
- Salt & black pepper, to taste
- 32g fresh parsley, chopped

Directions:

1. Add all the fixings to your slow cooker.
2. Cover with its lid and cook on low for 4 hours. Stir well and serve.

Nutrition: Calories: 376; Carbs: 57g; Fat: 22g; Protein: 33g

Creamy Tomato Soup

Preparation time: 15 minutes
Cooking time: 2-3 hours
Servings: 8
Ingredients:

- 15ml olive oil
- 1 onion, chopped
- 2 cloves garlic, peeled and crushed
- 1 yellow pepper, sliced
- 1 stick celery, finely chopped
- 200g fresh beef tomatoes, quartered
- Half (400g) can of chopped tomatoes
- 5g brown sugar
- 5g black pepper
- 5g dried herbs

Directions:

1. Heat the olive oil in your frying pan and cook the onions and garlic over medium heat for 8-10 until the onions have softened and caramelized.
2. Place the onions and garlic into the slow cooker and the remaining ingredients. Cover with its lid and cook for 2-3 hours.
3. Transfer it to your blender and blend until smooth. Top with some extra herbs or cheese. Serve.

Nutrition: Calories: 230; Carbs: 17g; Fat: 17g; Protein: 9g

Spicy Potato Soup

Preparation time: 15 minutes
Cooking time: 5-10 hours
Servings: 6-8
Ingredients:

- 450g minced beef or sausages, browned
- 900g cubed peeled potatoes
- 1 small onion, chopped
- 675ml tomato sauce
- 2 tsp salt
- ½ tsp pepper
- ½ tsp hot pepper sauce
- Water, as needed

Directions:

1. Combine all the fixings except water in the slow cooker. Add enough water to cover the ingredients.
2. Cover with its lid and cook on low for 8 to 10 hours, or on high for 5 hours, until potatoes are tender.

Nutrition: Calories: 159; Carbs: 16g; Fat: 5g; Protein: 12g

Corn Chowder

Preparation time: 15 minutes
Cooking time: 6-7 hours & 10 minutes
Servings: 4

Ingredients:

- 6 slices bacon, diced
- 115g chopped onions
- 450g diced peeled potatoes
- 285g frozen sweetcorn
- 450g cream-style corn or canned sweetcorn
- 1 tbsp sugar
- 1 tsp Worcestershire sauce
- 1 tsp seasoned salt
- ¼ tsp pepper
- 250ml water

Directions:

1. In a skillet or frying pan, cook the bacon for 5 minutes until crisp. Remove excess oil.
2. Add the onions and potatoes to your frying pan and sauté for 5 minutes. Drain well.
3. Combine all the fixings in your slow cooker. Cover with its lid and cook on low for 6 to 7 hours. Serve.

Nutrition: Calories: 140; Carbs: 29g; Fat: 2g; Protein: 2g

Beef And Vegetable Stew

Preparation time: 15 minutes
Cooking time: 5 hours & 15 minutes
Servings: 4
Ingredients:

- 30ml olive oil
- 1 onion, chopped
- ½ spring onion, chopped
- 1 clove garlic, chopped
- 2 large carrots, chopped into small chunks
- 1 large leek, chopped finely
- 2 celery sticks, chopped finely
- Half (200g) can of chopped tomatoes
- 30 g tomato puree
- A handful of fresh thyme
- A handful of fresh parsley
- 2 beef stock cubes, crushed
- 800g beef, diced

Directions:

1. Heat 15ml oil in a frying pan and add the onion, spring onion, and garlic. Cook them for 5-6 minutes until the onions start to caramelize.
2. Add the carrots, leeks, and celery, then cook for a few minutes.
3. Transfer this mixture into the slow cooker with the chopped tomatoes, tomato puree, fresh herbs, and beef stock cubes.
4. Heat the remaining 15ml of oil in the frying pan and add the beef. Cook for 8 minutes until it is cooked through.
5. Transfer the beef to your slow cooker and add enough water. Leave the mixture to cook for 5 hours, stirring occasionally. Serve.

Nutrition: Calories: 564; Carbs: 35g; Fat: 24g; Protein: 39g

Seafood Stew

Preparation time: 10 minutes
Cooking time: 2 hours & 30 minutes
Servings: 4
Ingredients:

- 1 (795 g) can tomatoes, crushed
- 15g tomato paste
- 1-litre vegetable broth
- 3 garlic cloves, minced
- 120g white onion, diced
- 5g thyme, dried
- 5g dried basil
- 5g oregano, dried
- 2.5g celery salt
- 1.25g red pepper flakes, crushed
- 0.625g cayenne pepper

- Salt & pepper, to taste
- 455g large shrimp
- 455g scallops
- A handful of fresh parsley, chopped

Directions:
1. Add all the fixings, except seafood, into the slow cooker. Cover with its lid and cook on low for 2 hours.
2. Stir in the seafood and continue cooking on low for 30 minutes. Serve warm.

Nutrition: Calories: 335; Carbs: 2g; Fat: 5g; Protein: 18g

Green Chilli Stew

Preparation time: 15 minutes
Cooking time: 4-6 hours
Servings: 6-8
Ingredients:
- 3 tbsp oil
- 2 garlic cloves, minced
- 1 large onion, diced
- 450g minced sirloin
- 250g minced pork
- 750ml chicken broth or stock
- 500ml water
- 2 (113g) cans of diced green chillies
- 4 large potatoes, diced
- 285g frozen sweetcorn
- 1 tsp black pepper
- 1 tsp crushed dried oregano
- ½ tsp ground cumin
- 1 tsp salt

Directions:
1. Cook the onion, garlic, sirloin, and pork in oil in a skillet. Cook for 10 minutes until the meat is no longer pink.
2. Combine all the fixings in your slow cooker. Cover with its lid and cook on low for 4 to 6 hours or until potatoes are soft.

Nutrition: Calories: 75; Carbs: 10g; Fat: 3g; Protein: 2g

Fajita Stew

Preparation time: 15 minutes
Cooking time: 6-8 hours & 20 minutes
Servings: 8
Ingredients:
- 1.1kg boneless beef topside or silverside steak, trimmed excess fat & cut into 2-inch pieces
- 1 onion, chopped
- 1 envelope dry fajita seasoning mix (about 2 tablespoons)
- 1 (400g) can of chopped tomatoes, undrained
- 1 red pepper, cut into 1-inch pieces
- 60g flour
- 60ml water

Directions:
1. Combine the beef and onion in your slow cooker. Mix the fajita seasoning and undrained tomatoes. Pour it over the beef.
2. Place the peppers on top, cover with its lid, and cook on low for 6 to 8 hours or until beef is tender.
3. Combine the flour and water in a small bowl. Gradually add to the slow cooker. Cover with its lid and cook on high for 15 to 20 minutes until thickened, stirring occasionally.

Nutrition: Calories: 208; Carbs: 7g; Fat: 10g; Protein: 23g

Hungarian Barley Stew

Preparation time: 20 minutes
Cooking time: 5 hours & 13 minutes
Servings: 8
Ingredients:

- 2 tbsp oil
- 680g diced beef
- 2 large onions, diced
- 1 medium green pepper, chopped
- 2 (400g) can of whole tomatoes
- 115g ketchup
- 150g dry small pearl barley
- 1 tsp salt
- .½ tsp pepper
- 1 tbsp paprika
- 285g frozen baby butter beans
- 750ml water
- 250ml sour cream

Directions:

1. Cook the diced beef in oil in your frying pan for 8 minutes. Add the onions and green peppers, then sauté for 5 minutes.
2. Pour it into the slow cooker and add the remaining ingredients except sour cream. Cover with its lid and cook on high for 5 hours. Stir in the sour cream before serving.

Nutrition: Calories: 486; Carbs: 84g; Fat: 5g; Protein: 30g

Sweet Potato Lentil Stew

Preparation time: 15 minutes
Cooking time: 5-6 hours
Servings: 6
Ingredients:

- 1-litre fat-free vegetable broth or stock
- 675g sweet potatoes, peeled and cubed
- 350g lentils, rinsed
- 3 medium carrots, cut into 1-inch pieces
- 1 medium onion, chopped
- 4 garlic cloves, minced
- ½ tsp ground cumin
- ¼ tsp ground ginger
- ¼ tsp cayenne pepper
- 60g minced fresh coriander or parsley
- ¼ tsp salt

Directions:

1. Combine all the fixings except the coriander and salt in your slow cooker. Cook on low for 5 to 6 hours or until vegetables are tender. Stir in the coriander and salt just before serving.

Nutrition: Calories: 300; Carbs: 30g; Fat: 3g; Protein: 14g

APPETIZERS

Garlic Herb Mashed Potatoes

Preparation time: 10 minutes
Cooking time: 2 hours
Servings: 6

Ingredients:

- 1.1kg baking or red potatoes, cut into small chunks
- 130g sour cream or plain yoghurt
- 110ml whole milk
- 70g butter
- 4 garlic cloves, minced
- 15g parsley
- 1.25g oregano

Directions:

1. Add the potatoes to a greased slow cooker. Cover with its lid and cook on high within 2 hours.
2. Add the remaining fixings, and flavour it with salt plus pepper. Mash the potatoes and fully combine them with all other ingredients. Serve.

Nutrition: Calories: 168; Carbs: 8g; Fat: 15g; Protein: 3g

Tomato Beef Nachos

Preparation time: 10 minutes
Cooking time: 4-6 hours
Servings: 20
Ingredients:

- 950g minced beef
- 1 can pinto beans in tomato sauce
- 1½ tbsp brown sugar
- 1 tbsp cider vinegar
- 2 tsp ground coriander
- 1 tsp cayenne pepper
- 2 tbsp chilli powder
- 2 tsp ground cumin
- 2 tsp dried oregano
- ¾ tsp salt
- Tortilla chips, cheddar, lettuce, and sour cream to serve

Directions:

1. Combine the beef, pinto beans, chilli powder, sugar, cumin, coriander, oregano, and cayenne pepper in the slow cooker.
2. Cook for 4 to 6 hours on low until the meat crumbles. Add the vinegar plus salt, then mix it well. Serve it with cheese, tortilla chips, lettuce, and sour cream.

Nutrition: Calories: 107; Carbs: 3g; Fat: 3g; Protein: 14g

Apricot Glazed Carrots

Preparation time: 15 minutes
Cooking time: 6-7 hours
Servings: 6
Ingredients:

- 900g small carrots
- 100g butter
- 60g peach or apricot preserves
- 50g brown sugar
- 30g cornstarch
- 30ml water
- 1.25ml balsamic vinegar
- 1.2g thyme

Directions:

1. Layer the small carrots at the bottom of the slow cooker.
2. Mix the fruit preserves, sugar, cinnamon, and butter in a bowl—season well with salt and pepper.
3. In a separate bowl or cup, stir together the cornstarch and water until combined, then mix into the buttery preserves mixture.
4. Pour the sauce over the carrots into the slow cooker. Cover with its lid and cook on low for 6-7 hours.

Nutrition: Calories: 220; Carbs: 24g; Fat: 14g; Protein: 2g

Cheesy Spinach

Preparation time: 5 minutes
Cooking time: 4 hours
Servings: 6
Ingredients:

- 550g spinach, chopped & thawed
- 300g cottage cheese
- 200g shredded cheddar cheese
- 50g butter
- 30g all-purpose flour
- 3 large eggs
- 2.5g garlic powder

Directions:

1. Combine all the ingredients in your bowl. Season it with salt and pepper.

2. Pour it into a greased slow cooker and cover. Cook on high for 1 hour. Adjust to low heat and cook for 3 more hours. Serve.

Nutrition: Calories: 311; Carbs: 10g; Fat: 21g; Protein: 21g

Chicken Mozzarella Meatballs

Preparation time: 15 minutes
Cooking time: 3 hours
Servings: 8
Ingredients:

- 2 (800g) cans of chopped tomatoes
- 450g ground chicken
- 350g mozzarella balls, drained
- 60ml red wine
- 60g grated parmesan cheese
- 60g breadcrumbs
- 3 garlic cloves, diced
- 1 large egg
- 1 medium onion, diced
- 2.5g basil
- 2.5g oregano

Directions:

1. Add the red wine, diced garlic, onion, and chopped tomatoes to the slow cooker—season with salt, pepper, and basil.
2. Combine the ground chicken, grated parmesan, egg, and breadcrumbs in your large bowl—season with salt, pepper, and oregano.

3. Once combined, flatten about 1g of the chicken mixture onto a clean surface. Add a mozzarella ball to the centre of the flattened meat and roll it into a ball.
4. Repeat with the remaining chicken and mozzarella. Place the rolled meatballs into the slow cooker. Cover with its lid and cook on high for 3 hours. Serve with any extra parmesan or basil.

Nutrition: Calories: 326; Carbs: 12g; Fat: 16g; Protein: 32g

Creamed Corn with Bacon

Preparation time: 5 minutes
Cooking time: 3 hours
Servings: 6

Ingredients:
- 6 (1.2kg) cans of sweet corn
- 220g cream cheese
- 100ml milk
- 100ml double cream
- 100g butter
- 3 bacon strips, cooked & crumbled
- 1 spring onion, finely chopped
- 15g granulated sugar

Directions:
1. Mix all the fixings in the slow cooker except for the bacon and onion—season with salt plus black pepper. Stir to combine.
2. Cover with its lid and cook on high for 3 hours. Shortly before cooking time is complete, uncover and stir well.
3. Scatter the bacon bits all over the cooked creamed corn. Serve with a topping of spring onions.

Nutrition: Calories: 351; Carbs: 10g; Fat: 34g; Protein: 5g

Mixed Nuts

Preparation time: 10 minutes
Cooking time: 3 hours
Servings: 10
Ingredients:
- 300g mixed nuts (almonds, cashews, pecans, walnuts, Brazil nuts)
- 100g brown sugar
- 75ml honey or maple syrup
- 15g cinnamon
- 10g vanilla extract
- 50ml water

Directions:
1. Mix all the fixings in a bowl except the water.
2. Place the nut mixture in the slow cooker and pour over the water until they are evenly coated.
3. Put the lid on and then cook on low for 3 hours until the pecans are crisp and crunchy. Serve.

Nutrition: Calories: 199; Carbs: 13g; Fat: 18g; Protein: 12g

Cheesy Onions

Preparation time: 10 minutes
Cooking time: 2-4 hours
Servings: 6-8

Ingredients:
- 680g small onions, peeled
- 4 slices bacon, cooked and crumbled

- 1 (300g) can of Cheddar cheese soup
- 120ml milk
- 20g grated Parmesan cheese

Directions:
1. Place the whole onions in your slow cooker.
2. Mix the remaining ingredients in your bowl and pour it into a slow cooker. Gently mix it well.
3. Cook on high for 2 hours or low for 4 hours until onions are fully tender.

Nutrition: Calories: 270; Carbs: 10g; Fat: 23g; Protein: 8g

Sweet Potato Wedges

Preparation time: 10 minutes
Cooking time: 4 hours
Servings: 8
Ingredients:
- 600g sweet potato, cut into wedges
- 100g butter, melted
- 30g brown sugar
- 5g cinnamon
- 5g nutmeg
- 5g black pepper

Directions:
1. Place your potato wedges in a bowl and pour over the melted butter. Stir until the potatoes are fully covered.
2. Sprinkle the sugar and spices, then toss until the seasoning is evenly spread across the potatoes.

3. Transfer the potatoes to your slow cooker, add the lid, and cook on a high heat for 4 hours until the potatoes are fully cooked through.

Nutrition: Calories: 282; Carbs: 25g; Fat: 5g; Protein: 7g

Bavarian Cabbage

Preparation time: 10 minutes
Cooking time: 3-8 hours
Servings: 4-8
Ingredients:
- 1 small head of red cabbage, sliced
- 1 medium onion, chopped
- 3 tart apples, cored and quartered
- 2 tsp salt
- 240ml hot water
- 2 tbsp sugar
- 80ml vinegar
- 3 tbsp bacon drippings

Directions:
1. Place all the fixings in the slow cooker.
2. Cover with its lid and cook on low for 8 hours or on high for 3 hours. Stir well before serving.

Nutrition: Calories: 126; Carbs: 13g; Fat: 7g; Protein: 5g

Spinach & Artichoke Dip

Preparation time: 10 minutes

Cooking time: 2 hours & 30 minutes

Servings: 12

Ingredients:

- 1 (500g) can of artichoke hearts sliced into quarters
- 400g spinach
- 400g cream cheese
- 300ml plain Greek yoghurt or sour cream
- 100g shredded mozzarella or cheddar cheese
- 100g grated parmesan cheese
- 2 garlic cloves, minced
- 1 red onion, diced

Directions:

1. Add all the fixings to the slow cooker—season well with salt and black pepper. Stir to combine.
2. Cover with its lid and cook on low for 2 hours. Stir to mix around the cream cheese. Cook for an additional 30 minutes and serve.

Nutrition: Calories: 252; Carbs: 8g; Fat: 21g; Protein: 10g

Cheesy Sweetcorn

Preparation time: 10 minutes

Cooking time: 3-4 hours

Servings: 8

Ingredients:

- 500g frozen sweetcorn
- 400g cream cheese, cubed
- 4 tbsp butter
- 3 tbsp water
- 3 tbsp milk
- 2 tbsp sugar
- 225g grated Cheddar cheese

Directions:

1. Add all the fixings to the slow cooker and stir well.
2. Cover with its lid and cook on low for 3 to 4 hours. Stir well before serving.

Nutrition: Calories: 367; Carbs: 6g; Fat: 32g; Protein: 12g

Glazed Maple Sweet Potatoes

Preparation time: 10 minutes

Cooking time: 7-9 hours

Servings: 5

Ingredients:

- 5 medium sweet potatoes, cut into ½-inch-thick slices
- 55g brown sugar, packed
- 60g pure maple syrup
- 60ml apple cider
- 2 tbsp butter

Directions:

1. Place the sweet potatoes in your slow cooker.
2. Mix the brown sugar, maple syrup, and apple cider in a small bowl. Pour over potatoes and stir until all the sweet potato slices are covered.
3. Cover with its lid and cook on low for 7 to 9 hours or until potatoes are tender. Stir in butter before serving.

Nutrition: Calories: 197; Carbs: 25g; Fat: 11g; Protein: 2g

DESSERTS

Chocolate And Peanut Butter Bites

Preparation time: 5 minutes
Cooking time: 2 hours
Servings: 20
Ingredients:
- 400g unsalted peanuts, chopped
- 400g milk chocolate
- 100g chocolate chips
- 400g peanut butter
- 30ml honey or maple syrup

Directions:
1. Grease the inner compartment of your slow cooker.
2. Mix all the fixings in a large bowl and transfer them into the slow cooker. Place the lid and turn it on low heat. Cook for 2 hours, stirring once every 30 minutes.
3. Remove the sweet and sticky mixture in small clusters using a spoon and place them on a baking sheet. Allow the clusters to cool for 1-2 hours. Store in the fridge or freezer before serving.

Nutrition: Calories: 231; Carbs: 19g; Fat: 15g; Protein: 8g

Sticky Ginger Cake

Preparation time: 10 minutes
Cooking time: 4 hours
Servings: 8
Ingredients:
- 200g unsalted butter, softened
- 150g caster sugar
- 50g muscovado sugar
- 4 eggs, beaten
- 200g self-raising flour
- 5g ginger
- 5g nutmeg
- 20g crystallized ginger, chopped into small pieces
- 15ml golden syrup

Directions:
1. Grease your slow cooker's inside with butter or oil, or line it with parchment paper.
2. Mix the butter with both types of sugar until combined.
3. Fold in the eggs, followed by flour, spices, crystallized ginger, and golden syrup. Stir until fully combined.
4. Pour the mixture into your slow cooker, cover it with its lid, and turn on low heat.
5. Cook for 4 hours until the cake is cooked. Let it cool and serve with a drizzle of maple syrup!

Nutrition: Calories: 325; Carbs: 31g; Fat: 24g; Protein: 15g

Apple Crumble

Preparation time: 10 minutes
Cooking time: 3 hours & 30 minutes
Servings: 4
Ingredients:
- 5 Granny Smith apples, peeled and cored & sliced into wedges
- 1 orange, zested and half juiced
- 90g unsalted butter, melted
- 85g light muscovado sugar
- 75g plain flour
- 60g rolled oats
- 50g walnut pieces
- 1 tsp ground cinnamon

- ½ tsp ground ginger

Directions:
1. Mix the apples, ground cinnamon, orange zest and 1 tbsp juice in your bowl. Transfer to your slow cooker.
2. Process the oats and walnuts in your food processor until coarsely chopped. Transfer it to your bowl with the ginger, flour, sugar, and butter. Mix it well.
3. Spoon this mixture into your slow cooker until all apples are covered. Arrange two sheets of kitchen paper on top and cook on low for 3 hours and 30 minutes.
4. Discard the kitchen paper and cook for 10 minutes with the lid slightly open.

Nutrition: Calories: 519; Carbs: 63g; Fat: 29g; Protein: 5g

Easy Brownies

Preparation time: 15 minutes
Cooking time: 6 hours
Servings: 16
Ingredients:
- 1 (500g) pack of brownie mix
- 4 tbsp margarine or butter, melted
- 80–160g chopped walnuts

Directions:
1. Make the brownie mix as stated in the package directions, adding margarine and walnuts.

2. Pour the batter into a greased 7-inch (18cm) springform pan and place on the rack in a 5-6.5 litre slow cooker.
3. Cover with its lid and cook on high for 6 hours. Let it cool, remove, and cut into squares before serving.

Nutrition: Calories: 249; Carbs: 34g; Fat: 14g; Protein: 3g

Salted Caramel Bars

Preparation time: 10 minutes
Cooking time: 2-3 hours
Servings: 8
Ingredients:
- 100g butter
- 200g sugar
- 5g vanilla extract
- 1 egg, beaten
- 400g plain flour
- 100g caramel chocolate
- 2.5g sea salt

Directions:
1. Grease your slow cooker using butter or oil.
2. Mix the butter, sugar, and vanilla extract until fluffy. Whisk in the eggs until fully combined.
3. Gradually add the flour, constantly stirring to mix. Press half of the doughy mixture into the bottom of the slow cooker and even out the top.
4. Break up the caramel chocolate into small chunks and lightly press half of them into the base layer of dough.
5. Add the second half of the doughy mixture on top, followed by the remaining caramel chocolate chunks. Sprinkle the sea salt, and close with the lid.
6. Cook on low for 2-3 hours. Once cooked, remove from the slow cooker, and leave to cool on a drying rack. Cut into bars and serve.

Nutrition: Calories: 456; Carbs: 45g; Fat: 23g; Protein: 5g

Baked Stuffed Apples

Preparation time: 10 minutes
Cooking time: 2 hours & 30 minutes
Servings: 5

Ingredients:
- 5 red apples, cored
- 60g melted butter
- 60g brown sugar
- 50g old-fashioned oats
- 40g chopped pecans
- 5g ground cinnamon
- 100ml water

Directions:
1. With a knife, create a wider well at the top of the apple, and remove its flesh.
2. In a bowl, combine the butter, oats, chopped pecans, ground cinnamon, sugar, and a pinch of salt.
3. Stuff this mixture inside your empty apples, pressing it down. Pour water into the slow cooker, then set down the stuffed apples inside.
4. Cover with its lid and cook on high for 2 hours and 30 minutes. Serve.

Nutrition: Calories: 342; Carbs: 51g; Fat: 17g; Protein: 3g

Chocolate Caramel Cake

Preparation time: 10 minutes
Cooking time: 6 hours
Servings: 8

Ingredients:
- 1 (400g) can of condensed milk, remove the paper label
- 200g plain flour
- 100g sugar
- 45g cocoa powder
- 5g baking powder
- 200 of any milk of your choice
- 45ml olive oil
- 5g vanilla extract
- 150g milk chocolate, chopped
- 100ml double cream

Directions:
1. Place the can of condensed milk in a stockpot. Fill the stockpot with around 5cm of water and let it boil. Simmer for 3 hours to caramelize the milk.
2. Grease the inner component of the slow cooker or line it with parchment paper.
3. Whisk the flour, sugar, cocoa powder, plus baking powder in your bowl. Add the milk, olive oil, vanilla extract, and chocolate to the bowl, then stir to form a cake batter. Pour it into your slow cooker.
4. Mix the caramelized condensed milk and double cream in your bowl, then transfer it to the slow cooker. Cover with its lid and cook on high for 3 hours. Serve.

Nutrition: Calories: 576; Carbs: 49g; Fat: 42g; Protein: 8g

Sticky Date Pudding

Preparation time: 30 minutes
Cooking time: 5 hours
Servings: 6

Ingredients:
- 250g pitted dates, chopped
- 5g baking soda
- 100g unsalted butter, softened
- 200g granulated sugar
- 5g vanilla extract
- 2 eggs, beaten
- 350g self-raising flour
- 150g brown sugar
- 45ml golden syrup

Directions:
1. Mix the dates, baking soda, and 300ml boiling water in a bowl.
2. Mix the butter, granulated sugar, and vanilla extract in another bowl until fluffy. Fold in the beaten eggs, flour, and dates mixture.
3. Grease the slow cooker or line it with parchment paper. Pour the sticky date batter, brown sugar, and golden syrup into the slow cooker.
4. Pour 750ml boiling water into the slow cooker on top. Place the lid and cook on low heat for 4 hours. Serve.

Nutrition: Calories: 599; Carbs: 67g; Fat: 33g; Protein: 8g

Crème Brulé

Preparation time: 5 minutes
Cooking time: 2 hours
Servings: 6
Ingredients:
- 3 egg yolks
- 100ml whipping cream
- 100g sugar
- 5g vanilla extract

Directions:
1. Combine the egg yolks, whipping, 50g sugar, and vanilla extract in a bowl.
2. Place two rolls of tin foil into the bottom of your slow cooker and place 6 ramekins between the two lines of tin foil to secure them.
3. Pour enough boiling water into the slow cooker to fill it to about one-third of the way up the ramekins.
4. Place the lid and then turn it on to low heat. Cook for 2 hours until the custard topping is set.
5. Remove the ramekins and leave them to set for around 6 hours.
6. Sprinkle with a bit of extra sugar and lightly torch using a culinary torch until the sugar on the top turns brown.

Nutrition: Calories: 486; Carbs: 27g; Fat: 31g; Protein: 4g

Blueberry Cobbler

Preparation time: 10 minutes
Cooking time: 4 hours
Servings: 6 servings
Ingredients:

- 600g blueberries
- 250ml whole milk
- 180g all-purpose flour
- 150g granulated sugar
- 60g softened butter
- 30g cornstarch
- 15g baking powder
- 10g ground cinnamon
- 5g vanilla extract

Directions:

1. In a bowl, sift together the flour and baking powder. Add two-thirds sugar, softened butter, and a pinch of salt. Stir in the milk and mix slowly to prevent clumps from forming.
2. Mix the remaining one-third sugar, vanilla extract, ground cinnamon, and blueberries in a separate bowl.
3. Add the batter to the greased slow cooker in an even layer. Top with sugar-coated blueberries. Cook on low for 4 hours and serve.

Nutrition: Calories: 374; Carbs: 69g; Fat: 10g; Protein: 5g

Candied Nuts

Preparation time: 10 minutes
Cooking time: 2-4 hours
Servings: 12
Ingredients:

- 55g butter
- 75g icing sugar
- 1½ tsp ground cinnamon
- ¼ tsp ground ginger
- ¼ tsp ground allspice
- 175g pecans
- 175g walnuts
- 125g unblanched almonds

Directions:

1. Mix the butter, sugar, and spices in a greased slow cooker. Add the nuts and toss to coat.
2. Cook on low for 2 to 4 hours until the nuts are crisp, stirring once during the cooking time. Let it cool and serve or store.

Nutrition: Calories: 327; Carbs: 11g; Fat: 31g; Protein: 6g

Triple Chocolate Brownies

Preparation time: 15 minutes
Cooking time: 3 hours
Servings: 20
Ingredients:

- 300g plain flour
- 150g cocoa powder
- 2.5g baking powder
- 75g unsalted butter
- 100g milk chocolate
- 100g dark chocolate
- 100g sugar
- 3 eggs, beaten
- 5g vanilla extract
- 100g white chocolate chips

Directions:

1. Lightly grease your slow cooker.
2. Whisk the flour, cocoa powder, plus baking powder in a bowl.
3. Place the butter, milk chocolate, and dark chocolate in a large pan and lightly heat until melted.

4. Turn off the heat and pour the sugar into the butter and chocolate mix. Add the eggs, vanilla, and chocolate chips.
5. Stir the flour mixture into the pan until fully combined. Transfer into the slow cooker and smooth out the top.
6. Place the lid and cook the brownie mixture on low heat for 3 hours. Leave to cool on a drying rack before cutting into squares.

Nutrition: Calories: 312; Carbs: 30g; Fat: 26g; Protein: 12g

Cherry Cobbler

Preparation time: 10 minutes
Cooking time: 2-5 hours & 30 minutes
Servings: 6-8

Ingredients:
- 1 (595 g) can of cherry pie filling
- 220 g dry cake mix of your choice
- 1 egg
- 3 tbsp evaporated milk
- ½ tsp cinnamon
- Non-stick cooking spray

Directions:
1. Lightly spray the slow cooker with non-stick cooking spray. Place the pie filling in your slow cooker and cook on high for 30 minutes.
2. Meanwhile, mix the remaining ingredients in your bowl until crumbly. Spoon onto the hot pie filling.
3. Cover with its lid and cook on low for 2 to 5 hours. Serve warm or cooled.

Nutrition: Calories: 350; Carbs: 56g; Fat: 13g; Protein: 2g

Sweet Rice Pudding

Preparation time: 10 minutes
Cooking time: 2 hours & 30 minutes
Servings: 6

Ingredients:
- 1 tsp butter
- 1 litre of semi-skimmed milk
- 200g wholegrain rice
- Small grating of nutmeg or cinnamon
- Honey, toasted almonds, and fruit to serve

Directions:
1. Grease the slow cooker all over the base and halfway up the sides. Heat the milk to a simmering point.
2. Mix the rice with the milk and pour it into the slow cooker. Add the nutmeg or cinnamon.
3. Cook for 2½ hours on high and stir once or twice if you can. Serve with honey, almonds, or fruit if you like.

Nutrition: Calories: 200; Carbs: 32g; Fat: 4g; Protein: 8g

Chunky Cranberry Applesauce

Preparation time: 15 minutes
Cooking time: 3-4 hours
Servings: 6

Ingredients:

- 6 baking apples, peeled or unpeeled, cut into 1-inch cubes
- 120ml apple juice
- 65g fresh or frozen cranberries
- 50g sugar
- ¼ tsp ground cinnamon (optional)

Directions:

1. Combine all the fixings in your slow cooker.
2. Cover with its lid and cook on low for 3 to 4 hours or until apples are as soft as you like them. Serve warm, or refrigerate and serve chilled.

Nutrition: Calories: 87; Carbs: 23g; Fat: 0g; Protein: 1g

Conclusion

Making healthy meals in a slow cooker is the simplest way to get a nutritious and delicious meal on the table with the least amount of effort. It is also a great way to save money by cooking in bulk and using leftovers throughout the week. With this cookbook, you will find recipes for all your favourite comfort foods that have been lightened up and made healthier, so you can feel good about eating them.

By cooking in bulk and using leftovers throughout the week, you can save money on your grocery bill. And because slow cooker recipes tend to be very easy to prepare, you will save time in the kitchen as well.

Foods cooked in a slow cooker—especially the recipes in this book—are not only healthy, but they are also packed with flavour. The slow cooking process allows the flavours of the ingredients to meld together, creating a rich and complex flavour that is often missing in quick, stovetop recipes. In addition to the amazing flavour, slow cooker recipes are also incredibly easy to make. With just a few minutes of prep time, you can set it and forget it, and come home to a delicious and healthy meal that's ready to eat.

We hope it has been helpful having this cookbook as a resource and that you will find the recipes herein not only healthy but also flavourful and easy to prepare. Cooking at home is a great way to eat healthy, save money, and spend time with loved ones. So, get cooking and enjoy!

Printed in Great Britain
by Amazon

14076301R00045